Seeing Through Blindness

Matt Harris

Seeing Through Blindness
2nd Edition
Published by Matt Harris
7867 Crilley Road
Glen Burnie, MD 21060

June 20, 2015

ISBN-13: 978-0692476109
ISBN-10: 0692476105

Dates, places, and events in this story are factual. Some fictional names were invented, and some details altered, to protect the privacy of those who were actually involved. Composites from several different people were also created to further protect privacy and to help move the narrative along.

Printed in the United States of America

To book Matt for a speaking and reciting engagement, or to discuss his book, please contact him at

matt@seeingthroughblindness.com

For more information about Matt's work, please visit

www.seeingthroughblindness.com

Because of the dynamic nature of the Internet, any web addresses or links contained in this book may have changed since publication and may no longer be valid.

To My Lovely Daughters,

Julia & Abby

Contents

Introduction

Since some material in this work needed updating, I am presenting this second edition of *Seeing Through Blindness.* It is the fourth book I have written so far, and it tells about my battles with blindness, with drugs, and with God, during my teenage years and young adult life. *Seeing Through Blindness* almost did not get written because, as a rule, I usually do not write about myself. I amended that "rule" several years ago, however, after telling my story to a group of about 80 teenagers at a church one night.

By then, I used a white cane because I had lost 99% of my eyesight. So I began my talk by sharing with the teenagers how, between the ages of 11 and 21, doctors kept telling me nothing was wrong with my eyes. But at the same time, I was struggling with symptoms from an undiagnosed eye disease called Retinitis Pigmentos—or RP for short.

I told the kids how RP is incurable and causes night blindness, severe loss of peripheral vision, and extreme sensitivity to sunlight. It can also eventually lead to complete blindness. I further explained how RP is such a confusing disease that a person could be diagnosed with it, be declared legally blind because of it, and still have 20/20 vision. That is exactly what happened to me at age 21.

I continued by telling the teens how tormented I was as a kid because I knew something was terribly wrong with my eyes. But no one believed me. I was also further tormented because, since no one understood the severity of my eye problem, I was expected to function as a normal sighted person—but failed miserably.

Then I discussed with the group how I now regret that back then I had turned to drugs and alcohol to numb the pain associated with this torment. Without glamorizing my behavior, I explained to the teens how my poor choices led to three arrests and many encounters with police. I also added how my abuse of PCP and LSD had finally derailed me.

I then proceeded to share with the teens how I had hoped the MVA would discover what my eye problem might have been when I went to take my driving test. But when I passed the driving test at age 17, after my third attempt, my license carried no restrictions at all for my eyesight. Yet, despite what my license said, my "blindness" made it unsafe for me to drive at night or on unfamiliar roads during the day. After adding the MVA to the list of doctors who also could not find anything wrong with my eyes, I became a very frustrated and confused young man.

As I closed my talk that evening, you could hear a pin drop to the floor as I told this great group of kids how Jesus had changed me after I asked Him to come into my life and save me on December 12, 1982. Then, after sharing a brief gospel message with the teens, twelve of them gave their lives to Jesus Christ. It was the same church where I had accepted Christ 30 years earlier, Lake Shore Baptist.

The next day, after realizing the impact my story had on these teenagers, I started writing *Seeing Through Blindness*. And since its first publication, the book has opened up many doors for me to bring awareness to RP and to help people who are battling with blindness, drugs, and God.

Shortly after its publication, I adapted *Seeing Through Blindness* into a feature-length screenplay. And a portion of the script is currently in the preliminary stages of being produced into a short film.

***

2

Part One, Retinitis Pigmentosa (RP)

Allow me to introduce you to the beast
I once was, before I became this
new creature through the blood of God's Son.
Come and travel down the stairs of time with me,
but first, watch your step, and grab the railing please,
until we alight on the landing dated
August 21, 1981,
where I'll begin this tale of my dark daze
of drug abuse, blindness, and rebellion,
through which the Light of the world would shine on me!

"Matt Harris, Dr. Miller can see you now,"
my eye doctor's assistant tells me, her pupils
pecking over glasses set low on her nose.
For days, I'd already been waiting,
like a defendant for a verdict,
for the test results to determine
why my eyes had been so uncooperative
for the past ten years . . . since age eleven.

"Have a seat, Matt." Dr. Miller says.
"Your test results confirm what we discussed
on your initial visit with me.
You have Retinitis Pigmentosa—
or RP for short. It's incurable
and progressive, and, so far, has carved
eighty-two degrees from your visual field,
which puts you in the legally blind range—though
your acuity is still 20/20."

Dr. Miller diagnosed in ten minutes
what doctors for the past decade had missed!

Later that day, I surrender my cares:

3

Sliding an eight-track tape into its player,
"Born to be Wild" by Steppenwolf stirs,
as the third hit of weed from my bong explodes
inside my lungs. Immediately,
tentacles from THC tickle my brain,
as it cuts a swath through my synapses.
My black bucket seat absorbs me inside
the refuge of my '68 Mustang,
its *Firestones* eagerly awaiting
to leave their marks on asphalt once again
instead of idling in its current state,
sinking into leaves and twigs from oak trees,
that stand as stoic sentries to its prison:
the tangled woods behind my parent's house.
And although I've not driven my black beauty
for two years, still, whenever I clench the wheel,
and my key turns the engine into music,
in my imagination, I travel
to the outermost dimensions of my choosing.

My lack of funds is the excuse I use
to tell people why my Mustang has sat
corralled in the woods for the past two years.
The truth is I could not lie anymore,
at least not to myself, about the fact
that my eyes had become like sponges,
and some unknown entity had been wringing
peripheral vision from their field. Yet,
lying about it comforts me more than truth—
a weapon I learned to use to survive.
For a falsehood to convince, it commands
certain manipulative dexterities:
the two most essential skills for success are
a swift mind and a memory of stone,
upon which to chisel each fable on:
a data bank for future reference.

After my bong strikes me with two more hits,
torment chafes my mind over the thought of how
my memories are oftentimes much like
a burning building with me trapped inside.
As smoke begins to overwhelm me again,
I remember a time long ago, when,
even before my first RP symptom
pitched its tent to camp in my visual field,
white lies in my defective cones distorted
my own perception of what color was.
My parents told my fourth-grade teacher, Sister
Agnes Marie, about my colorblindness.
She promised to help and not to tell a soul.

But just like how air escapes from the mouth
of a balloon, so, too, my secret leaked.
So at recess a bully named Joseph Sear
chose to deride me in front of some kids:
"What color's this, blind as a bat Matt,"
he teased, while holding up different objects,
as other children joined in the fun with him.
Ashamed, I yelled and lied, "I'm not colorblind."
And when he refused to stop, I showed him
how bullies bleed just like the rest of us.

(Grandma taught me *that* when I was but four,
when a kid busted my lip with a swing
at a park in Curtis Bay. She grabbed me
and half dragged me to the drinking fountain,
where he had run to splash kids with some water.
"Take your fist, Matt," Grandma said, "and bash him
in the mouth." I always listened to Grandma.)

After I bashed Joseph Sear with my fist,
I would have sworn his blood looked brown to me.

And though Joseph Sear never asked me
what the color of something was again,
he became what most fallen bullies become: a *victim*.
After squealing like a little girl to Sister Agnes Marie,
that I'd hit him, and that I'd lied about my colorblindness,
she hit me with a punch harder than any
that a playground bully could have mustered.

In front of my fourth grade class, she tested me
to see if I *really* was colorblind.
Clenching her wooden pointer, she waddled
to the bulletin board, where hot air balloons,
our class had fashioned from construction paper,
hung lazily, stapled to the sky.

"What color is this one, Matt?" She asked,
while tapping her pointer on a balloon.
"And don't lie!"
My ears burned with an anger
that would be my unwelcomed guest for years.
"Joseph made fun of me. That's why I lied!"
I cried while balloons blurred through my tears.

I put so much time and money into
my Mustang. And for what? I ask myself,
as I replace Steppenwolf with Fleetwood Mac,
and space out on the smoke that rises
from the half inch of ash that quivers
on the *Salem* lounging in its ashtray,
as if it has answers to some mystery.
While I chew on my diagnosis,
like a piece of Wrigley's *Doublemint Gum*,
this epiphany floods me with some relief:
For the first time in ten years I know
what my problem is. Why is that funny?

If I had a belly, it would be jiggling!
I can't stop laughing. Why would I want to?
Is it the pot? No! It's this paradox:
a blind man with 20/20 vision!

Thunder only happens when it's raining,

Fleetwood Mac sings, smoothing out my buzz a bit.
My thunder started when I was eleven;
that's when symptoms from my RP first started.

* * *

Part Two, Diamond Daze

I'd heard how diamonds were a girl's best friend.
But when I was a boy, living in Baltimore,
I played inside a diamond so much so
that it became one of my very best friends,
as it encompassed me with all its brilliance.
In the neighborhood, we seldom were apart.
For years already, by age 11,
baseball had been like a brother to me.
Even the bios on the backs of baseball cards
tutored me in reading like a teacher,
resulting in a savant-like knowledge of
hundreds of players' batting averages,
ERAs, RBIs, and homerun totals.

It was spring, 1971. Yes!
And the Orioles were World Series champions,
having clobbered Cincinnati in the fall.
I grabbed my ball glove and bike and pedaled
over coarse concrete that wended its way
through blocks of bleak blue-collar brick row homes.
Old Bay seasoning, coating crabs while they steamed,
clawed at my nose,
its scent streaming through screened doors.
Hurried women hung wet wash on their clotheslines,
white linens waving like flags of surrender,
while, with a *Pabst* in one hand, and a *Pall Mall*
burning in the other, men rested
their tired forearms on chain-linked fences, talking
and laughing more loudly with each emptied *Pabst.*
This was home, the aroma of Lakeland.

As I steered my bike with its extended forks
into the park, drifting toward the diamond,

at ease on my brand new banana seat,
I heard that *screech*, a musical note to me,
when the barrel of an aluminum bat
introduced itself to a baseball,
and the applause that always followed,
either for the batter, when he reached base,
or for the fielder, when he threw him out.
The word *exhilaration* did not exist
in my decade-old vocabulary back in '71;
but now I know it expressed
how baseball once whirled inside me.

After chaining my bike to a lamppost,
I sneezed when I smelled the freshly cut grass
that pieced together our little league field.
"*Gesundheit*, Duck," my teammate, Nicholas, said,
while hustling out to field his first-base position.
We played on the same all-star squad last year,
where I'd gobbled up everything hit my way
at second base. I'd never felt more at home.
When practice started this year, that all changed,
as groundballs rolled right by me unnoticed.
I moved for line drives only when they hit me;
pop ups became like aerial assaults,
plunking me in the head so much
that eventually the sound of the bat striking the ball
conditioned me to duck. And, of course,
more often than not, the batter hit the ball elsewhere.
But since I'd still be ducking,
my teammates started to call me *Duck*.
I had no humor about it at all then;
in fact, their laughter knocked the wind from me
harder than an errant fastball to the back.
And just like how I battled to see a ball,
once it was launched from a baseball bat,

the eye doctors who would examine me
over the next decade also struggled
to diagnose my difficulty.

As opening day festivities began,
armies of families from the neighborhood
gathered with lounge chairs and charcoal grills,
that hurled their pleasant, scented gusts from scores
of hamburgers, *Esskay Franks*, and chicken legs,
while their envied juices trickled to the coals.
I found my niche, the bench, and stuck to it,
like the *P* on my cap that stood for Phillies.
I was becoming an outcast, more and more,
though still confident my problem would soon pass.
Maybe today I'll see the ball better,
I mused, after my coach, Mr. Don, yelled,
"Matt, since Chester ain't here yet, you're starting
in right field and you'll be batting ninth."

Although I'd been deported that year
from second base, and exiled to right field,
and fell from batting leadoff to hitting ninth,
nothing at that time could compare
to the feel of my sweaty fingers inside
the threadbare glove secured to my left hand.
Armed to the teeth with several pieces of
Bazooka Bubble Gum, I worked my molars
and my mandible, while bubbles bloomed and popped,
until the umpire shouted, *Play Ball!*

Our pitcher threw wildly, walking the first
three batters in a row on 12 straight pitches.
When Lou, batting cleanup, lumbered to the plate,
I began to pray,
"Dear God, please don't let him hit the ball my way."

But God said *No* to my prayer
and *Yes* to Lou Paul's instead.
Connecting with a gift our pitcher threw,
aluminum squealed *Hello* to the ball.

Deep to right, the blast sailed over my head;
I never saw it—not even a glimpse.
I heard it, though, rattle the rusty fence,
so I scanned its grassy bottom with my eyes.
I squinted and squinted, as Nicholas,
our first baseman, ran passed me. Shaking his head,
he growled through clenched teeth glinting with braces,
"You moron! What the heck's your problem, Matt?"
"Wish I knew," I said.
As he hurled the ball home,
the bases had emptied. Four runs had scored.

When Nicholas' gloved-hand struck my head,
it didn't hurt as much as the laughter from the stands.
So, there, in right field,
more than just a baseball disappeared,
as I swallowed my gum, my pride, and stood alone
like a blade of grass about to be mown.
For an edge of hardness began sharpening itself
on a whetstone inside me that day.
And back then,
it was too intangible for me to have dulled it.

* * *

Part Three, Still in the Mustang

Are magicians on the loose in my Mustang?
More than my eyesight seems to be vanishing.
Because after my last bong hit,
my reefer disappeared just like my *Doritos!*
Jeeter, my *pharmacist,* refers to it
as *Gungi Weed.* Jeeter bought a boatload,
metaphorically speaking, of course,
from some dreadlocked Jamaican dude new to town.
But any pothead worth a buzz always keeps
a stash to counter such acts of vanishing.
At the center of my steering wheel,
Ford engineered a nifty cover
that easily pries away, exposing a cylinder,
inside of which I store a spare supply of pot—
a favorite feature of mine I must admit.

I'm not surprised how RP has taken
its twisted finger and poked me in each eye.
Yet I had no idea my eyesight languished
in such an impoverished state as this.
It answers one question that has hounded me
like a pit bull chasing a Chihuahua:
No! I've not been crazy for the past decade,
yet many would have a sound argument
to the contrary. But, now, at least,
documentation exists as to why,
like an out-of-shape runner at a track meet
striving breathlessly to keep pace with the pack,
I've lagged behind my peers for ten years now,
academically, athletically, socially, and vocationally.

Yet, ironically, liberation lifts me,
like a man just freed from prison,

since my blindness can now be defined this day:
August 21, 1981.
Which reminds me, the O's and A's are playing,
with Jim Palmer and Rick Langford on the mound.

And no more *Rumors* from you, Fleetwood Mac.
Yes! I'm pulling the plug on that "Don't Stop" crap!
It sounds like a broken record after listening to it
at least a dozen times:

If you wake up and don't want to smile,
If it takes just a little while,
Open your eyes and look at the day;
You'll see things in a different way.

Don't stop, thinking about tomorrow.
Don't stop, it'll soon be here.
It'll be better than before.
Yesterday's gone; yesterday's gone.

Why not think about times to come,
And not about the things that you've done?
If your life was bad to you,
Just think what tomorrow will do . . . .

Okay, let's see, now, what will tomorrow do?
Bring me a day closer to complete darkness?
Or bring me a guide dog I can call *Buddy?*
Or even better yet, I know, how 'bout this:
a white cane in my hand to travel behind
to keep my dumb butt from bumping into stuff?
And how will I buy dope, much less feed *Buddy,*
when I join the unemployment club?
Yep, that's what *my* tomorrow will do!

But for today, I'll crack open this can

13

of ice-cold *Budweiser* from my cooler
to conquer my cotton mouth and wash away
the fuzz that clings to the walls of my throat.
Aah! There's my *Doritos,* right next to me,
hiding on the floor. Mmm! Nothing cures
my munchies like handfuls of *Doritos.*

What's up with this stupid static? I'm gonna miss
the first pitch. *Bash the dash.* Bam! Yep,
that always gets her tuned in real nice.
"No score after one," Chuck Thompson announces.
Stupid realtor commercial. I hate it!
It reminds me of when we moved from Lakeland
to out here in the boondocks of Pasadena.

* * *

Part Four, At Home

In the midst of Lakeland,
nestled on Norland Road,
surrounded by hundreds just like it,
our row home sat,
which I revered. Since age three, it sheltered me,
my mom, Mary, my dad, Jack, and my little sister, Cindy.
Candles from my fourteenth-birthday cake had been
snuffed out for only a few months
when the words *FOR SALE,* blasting like neon
from its *Doyle Realty* sign, blared at me
from their stake stabbed in the heart of my front yard.
I flipped my *Salem* at the smiling face
of the pretty woman plastered on the sign.
She took a direct hit to the forehead—
at least my aim was still on target.

After bicycling to the local store,
I tossed 42 cents onto the counter,
and snatched my cigarettes and some matches,
then pushed my way through the door of 7/11.
Before hopping back onto the seat of my bike,
I had to wait a few minutes, as always, till the sun stopped
suppressing my eyesight. Something similar to *whiteout*
occurred each time I exited a building into daylight.
And also whenever I entered a building,
my eyes called for a *timeout,* while I waited in darkness,
until they decided to adjust to the indoor lighting.
Whiteouts and *timeouts* lasted for several minutes,
and, of course, they were as foreign as French
to my friends. So frustration filled me,
like a rookie batting against Nolan Ryan,
when I lost step with them, while leaving,
or going into, houses, stores, or school.

15

I was falling behind in an ever
widening gap in a race with my peers.

In sync with the sun once again, I flew
across the parking lot, looking straight forward,
on a day more clear than plain English.
My handlebars rocked me in my ribcage,
like a solid left hook to the body,
as I crashed into the concrete wheel-stop
at the edge of a parking space, directly
in front of the Pantry Pride Supermarket.

My bicycle catapulted me headlong!

As I belly-flopped onto the black surface,
the sultry asphalt slapped me in the face.
After skidding to a stop like a *Goodyear*,
I was in a pile of pain like an untrained fighter
sprawled on the canvas down for the count.
Lacerations tattooed me from face to feet,
while my flesh sizzled from the road burn
like a French fry dipped into a deep fryer.
As I straightened my twisted handlebars,
my abrasions throbbed with every heartbeat,
while the polio of apathy hobbled
the hamstrings of slews of consumers, who,
ignorant of the term *Good Samaritan*,
begged off treading anywhere near my plight.
With another embarrassment behind me,
I lit my smoke and slung my match to the wind,
driving gingerly to the park, careful
not to allow any more *bumps* upend me along the way,
that, perhaps, my naked eye would not detect.

I had not been blinded to the fact how

I needed to concentrate more and more to see,
as less and less came into view.
And while this mystery speckled torment
throughout every region of my psyche,
my suffering alone in this manner
weighed down on me like a blacksmith's anvil.
As I attempted to forge a solution
to my ophthalmological problem,
which recently had even stumped the world famous
Wilmer Eye Institute at Johns Hopkins,
I drifted and entered into the park,
standing to pedal faster passed the diamond,
wishing the memory it still conjured up—
that fly ball three years ago I flubbed—
would crumble like clay I once kicked from my cleats.
I pulled onto the basketball court, which smelled
like ammonia from us boys using its walls
as urinals during our basketball games.

"Hey Jeeter, pass me the ball," I said.

Since age three, Jeeter Jones and I have been friends.
Right after we met, a piece of brick tested our friendship.
While acting like three-year-olds,
we fought over a toy dump truck. I pushed Jeeter,
and he would fall to the ground, then get up
and knock me to the ground. I would get up,
and the match continued, until his father,
who had a belly full of *Pabst,*
ordered his son to hit me with a piece of brick.
Jeeter obeyed his father for once.
Fortunately, God blessed me with a hard head.
But when my father heard how Mr. Jones
bragged to neighbors about his son's exploits,
he went down bent on bloodying Jeeter's dad.

Bang! Bang! Bang!
Dad rapped on Mr. Jones' door,
but like a boxer not answering the bell,
his rattling door was left unanswered. And, so,
no paddy wagon would need dispatching,
as my father's wrath finally subsided.

"Hey Matt, what happened to your face?" Jeeter asked,
while bounce passing a basketball my way.
"Chasing fly balls again, were you?" He needled.
"Still better lookin' than your mug," I said,
while swishing a jump shot from 20 feet.
"Yeah, I suppose that's why I'm with a hottie,
and you're with that skank named *nobody*.
"Shut up and give me the ball, moron," I said.
"Gotta match for this joint?" Jeeter asked.
I struck a flame and drew hard on the joint;
its buzz was direct and got right to the point.
Weed had become an herb in my garden.
My heart had already started to harden.

* * *

Part Five, Buzz Kill

Too bad my brain has a mind of its own!
Why did I let me talk myself into installing
this stereo system in my Mustang?
I didn't know what I was doing. But did that stop me?
No, of course not. So nothing but static now!

"We're in the home half of the second inning,"
Chuck Thompson's voice cracks from the radio,
"With the O's leading the A's 1-0,
Tony Armas takes Palmer's pitch for strike one."

As water in my bong starts bubbling again,
a whisper from *Budweiser* and weed entices me:
Drive! You can still do it. You'll be okay.

"Armas lines one! Snagged by Belanger at short,
who dove headlong to his left," Thompson exclaims,
interrupting my temptation for now.

"What's up, Willy? Outta weed again?" I ask.
"It's been dry, man. Do you have any, Matt?"
"Were ya not just engulfed in a cloud of it,
when ya opened my car door? Have a seat,
but don't sit your fat butt on my *Doritos*."

Willy Austin is an acquaintance,
someone I've tolerated but never really liked.
He's much more intelligent than he lets on
and likes to hit on other guys' girlfriends.
I don't mind sharing some weed with Willy,
but only every once in a while, though.

"Palmer misses with his fastball, walking

Cliff Johnson with two outs in the second.
That brings catcher Rick Dempsey to the mound
to chat with Palmer," Thompson tells us.

"Baseball's boring. I don't like it," Willy complains,
while some of my pot and one of my smokes
disappear into his lungs.
"When are you going to smoke *Marlboros*, Matt?
I can't stomach these nasty menthols of yours."

"You've been bummin' cigarettes from me
for seven years. Don't ya know by now
I only smoke *Salems* to tick your dumb,
redneck butt off? Ya moronic mooch!"

Pointing my middle finger at him, I say,

"Now, here's your map to the *Marlboro* store.
Ya got a lotta nerve, Willy. No,
ya can't have one of my beers. Besides,
aren't ya a *Miller* man, anyway?"
"No, Matt. I like *Budweiser*. You know that."
"Then grab me one too, ya jerk," I say.
"No! I'm not turning on 98 Rock!
And shut up about it already, will ya?
I don't even remember invitin' ya
over here to listen to the game with me!
Buzzkill! What's up with ya anyway?"

"Sell me a joint's worth of weed, Matt. Come on."
"I don't sell marijuana to narcs, ya fool."
"I'm not a narcotics officer, Matt.
You know that. I don't want people to think that."
"Hey, Willy, it's a joke. Lighten up!
And don't let the door hit ya in the rear end

on your way out. No! Ya can't have another
one of my *Budweisers* for the road."

Willy could have taken one of my Buds,
and, of course, I'd never have been the wiser—
and the cheesy pun is certainly intended!
But since he's in the dark about my blindness,
he doesn't know how my lack of sight offers much more
speed to his hand when considering this adage:
The hand is quicker than the eye!

I cling to secrecy for protection,
but for how long will my armor shield me?
Or is it a delusion, and, perhaps,
already as clear as a cloudless sky
to the outside world? Is the joke on me?
Since my albatross has been defined today,
I can reveal it and explain it. Right?

Wrong!

Secrecy is something I've held onto for too long.
Something I've earned. Something I've nurtured.
No one can have it. It's mine, at least for now.

* * *

Part Six, Sold Out

Just a few weeks after ninth grade started
at my new school, in Brooklyn, Maryland,
called Benjamin Franklin Junior High,
a crookedly placed decal that said *SOLD*
partially covered *FOR SALE* on the sign
in my front yard. The smile smeared on the face
of that woman glued to it seemed to have widened
in contrast to the frown that restricted mine.
Pasadena would soon be my new home.
Since drug use and the crime rate was rising,
faster than Tropical Storm Agnes had raised
her flood waters in 1972,
mom and dad, both filled with best intentions,
decided to throw my sister and me in a *U-Haul*
and drive us away, before the raging current
reached our front door. Too late!

I don't remember much about what I learned
in reading, writing, or arithmetic class.
Education consisted mostly of how
to shoulder myself through the idiocy
of racial tension, that seethed—like a pot
of grand mom's bubbling crab soup—through the halls
that snaked through Benjamin Franklin Junior High.
After entering school, on one sunny day,
I paused in the hallway to allow my eyes
a moment to recover from *timeout,*
while inadvertently impeding progress
of several schoolmates of mine. One of whom
literally kicked me in my butt and ordered,
gitcha white a** out the way.

Assailed by a din of Babel and darkness,

as the hall constricted me like a Python,
I kept my mouth shut and knife pocketed.
Sightless, it was useless as a drinking straw.
It was more of a security blanket
than a security measure. Anyway,
what I took away from class that day was this:
ignorance was a double-edged sword
that cuts both ways in regard to race.

That afternoon my newspapers arrived late;
and after my sister volunteered to help with them,
mom only further delayed us: "Matt, Cindy, come on,"
she yelled at us through our yard.
"Come in here and get ready for dinner."
"Wait a minute, mom.
We still have piles of papers to fold," I said.
"They can wait till after dinner," mom countered.
"The food's gonna get cold and dad's hungry."

I had delivered papers two years by then
for a Baltimore newspaper called *The News American.*
Dad and I connected somehow through my paper route,
since he also had one when he was a boy.
One fond memory I have was waking up early
on Sunday mornings to deliver newspapers with him.
After stacking my papers into an old wooden wagon,
and with our sweaty arms stained with their ink,
we pulled it along on its squeaky wheels,
which cried out in thirst for a sip of oil.
Some papers plopped on customers' doorsteps,
others slid to a stop at their *Welcome* mats.
And after the last paper plunked on its porch,
mom rewarded us with plates piled with pancakes.

"Go to war, Jack," mom hollered at my father,

sounding like the voice of Edith Bunker.
"You're not havin' chocolate puddin' for dinner again,
are ya? I got Irish Stew, ya know!"

This mixture of onions, spam, and potatoes
topped off our empty stomachs on many nights.
Mom tossed out her catchphrase, *Go to war, Jack,*
every time my dad did something that riled her.
I never learned the meaning of the term,
but I laughed, if not outwardly, then at least inwardly,
each time she would burst out with it.

"Ya want some more Irish Stew, Matt?" Mom offered,
while flitting about like a gnat,
already clearing the soiled dishes from the table.
"Sure, mom," I said, "I'm still starvin'. Pile it on!"

"We'll be movin' into our new house on November 30,"
dad candidly heralded between bites of buttered bread
and spoonfuls of piping hot chocolate pudding.
While my freshly filled plate of stew sat untouched,
I calculated the days remaining till
11/30/74.

The next day, I argued with my dad and said,
"I've already seen the place enough times.
I don't need to go again. We just went there
last weekend. I remember what it looks like!
I wanna play basketball here today. And besides,
we'll be livin' there soon enough.
I wanna enjoy the time I still have here."
"Ya can play basketball later," dad promised. "Let's go!"
On the way to tour our new neighborhood again,
the cancer of contempt spread through my smirk,
and no amount of chemo could cure it,

as the portrait of Lakeland faded
through the back window of my father's Ford.

Our new house was a split-foyer, single home.
It sat on a small peninsula
about a quarter mile from Grays Creek,
which was like a tongue that projected
from the mouth of the Magothy River
and licked the edge of our community.
Space crowded around our new house,
instead of other homes like how it was in Lakeland.
Thick woods stood out back, where an alley should run.
It was much too quiet and way too slow.
But this was where mom and dad had awakened
from their *American Dream.*   For years,
they sweated many hours laboring,
and so each of them deserved this higher rung
on the socio-economic ladder.
And although the perch wasn't *that* high up,
it was still high enough for my nose to bleed.

Only if clouds would rain some gas on this place,
and a lightning bolt would strike it like a match!
As my daydream stoked this inferno,
I pondered the path my footsteps treaded on,
while walking down my new street to the beach.
It was time for me to get used to this fork
I was forced to take onto Maryland Avenue,
where my new home was burning in my mind.
I dragged my feet on passed the baseball diamond,
vowing to myself never to play on it—
and not to voice how foul I was afield.
Crap! I cursed, when I clipped my kneecap
on a thin cable, barely visible,
threading its way through scores of pilings,

stationed around the borders of the beach.
I stepped on the pier and sat down on the dock,
dangling my feet just a foot above Grays Creek.

I fired up a *Salem* and took a deep drag;
the smoke mingled with salt air and creosote,
a pleasant scent in an odd sort of way.
Echoes throbbed in the air from a basketball,
bouncing from somewhere off in the distance.
Around the pier, it was like the inside of a bionic ear
that magnified sounds in the vast openness of the creek.
The volume from the once faint voices
of the basketball players suddenly increased
into what sounded like a screaming match.
A touch of Lakeland at last, I laughed,
while watching my *Salem* drown in Grays Creek.
"Time to go, Matt." Dad hollered from his Ford.
"We got a lotta packin' to do. Come on!"

* * *

Part Seven, Stairway to Heaven

My Mustang and I have this in common:
our luster continues to tarnish
like a corpse rotting in a casket!
As a mental mist clouds my memories,
my musing shifts back to present tense,
where RP cells have latched onto each retina
like a herd of ants ravaging a *Cheez-It*
that some careless hand let fall to the floor.
Dang if it ain't like I've spent twenty-one years
working out without having weights on the bar!
I can't even say *the world's passing me by,*
as I sit, bound to this seat, watching the world
stand still through my Mustang's sap-stained windshield,
while distortion overwhelms my perception.
As plume after plume of pot smoke wraps me
in its cancerous haze, the wind breathlessly moans
like a dying man's cries for his momma.

"A's 2, O's 1, with Al Bumbry batting
in the top of the third inning," Thompson says.
"Langford's curveball's low and away. Ball one."

Still staving off sobriety for now,
a glow shimmers from the belly of my bowl,
then fizzles out like fireworks on the Fourth,
as the smoke paws at my lungs like a bull
about to maul a clown at a rodeo.
I mute the game and slip Zeppelin in its sheath,
after the 8-track winds and jerks, out pours:

*There's a lady who's sure all that glitters is gold
And she's buying a stairway to heaven.*

Cranking up "Stairway to Heaven," I ponder

the surreal ride to work I had yesterday,
when that foul breath, that belched from Curtis Bay's
industrial throats, pressed upon us, while dad
drove me to my job at Graber's machine shop.
But while en route, my mind began to snore,
as dad sat behind the steering wheel
of his pulpit, preaching about God,
the Gospel, and some Book in the Bible
he referred to as Revelation.
Above the snores that thundered inside my head,
these lyrics from Rush the rock group whined,

My mind is not for rent to any god or government.

Dad, meanwhile, spun on, like a *Michelin*
down Curtis Avenue, explaining how
in the future seven years of Great
Tribulation would plague our planet, God
pouring out judgment from His cup of wrath
on populations, who, at that time,
will have turned away from Him to follow
Satan, his False Prophet, and Beast.
What on earth was dad talking about? I wondered
in the machine shop at lunchtime yesterday,
as I rested on my splintered workbench,
tired already from a morning of tasting
asbestos shavings from gasket making.
On the filter of my *Salem,* I smoked
and swilled some *Coke*, contemplating Christ,
clueless of His Second Coming, Salvation,
or any Great Tribulation—but my own.
Yet I heard Scripture whispering to me!

Ooh, it makes me wonder;
Ooh, it makes me wonder.

And though I'm not ready to open that Book,
the way I think about it and Christ have changed.
It intrigues me now how the Bible speaks
of the Second Coming of Jesus Christ—and
other future events it says will happen.
Dad told me, and not for the first time,
that Jesus loved me so much that He died
on the cross to forgive me of my sins.
I felt the love of Jesus yesterday
for the first time. He has my attention.
Dad said that if I repented from my sin—
agreed with God that I sinned against Him—
and believed that Jesus died on the cross for my sins,
and that God His Father raised Him from the dead,
He would save me from hell and give me eternal life.
All I had to do was call on His name.
I'm not ready for that commitment yet,
but I know I'm a sinner, that's obvious!

Yes, there are two paths you can go by,
but in the long run
There's still time to change the road you're on
Ooh, it makes me wonder
Ooh, Ooh, it makes me wonder

But mom raised me Catholic, took me to church.
I'm a born and bred Catholic boy, baptized
with holy water, made my first communion,
went to confession, and was confirmed—
an altar boy with eight years of Catholic school!
Yet emptiness overflows inside my soul.
Is it because Catholic boys need Jesus, too?

Religion never was important to dad.
That is until we relocated here—

to the suburbs in Pasadena—and he
started attending a church up the street:
Lake Shore Baptist. I've gone a few times.
Now, he's a freakin' deacon, of all things.
That's when he started telling not only me
but even all our neighbors about Jesus,
and only God knows who else. Embarrassing!
Couldn't he have taken up golf instead?

Your head is humming and it won't go,
in case you don't know
The piper's calling you to join him

Why do *I* have to face blindness, God?
I know life ain't fair. But this *really* ain't fair!
I wanna see a baseball hit from a bat,
and find a woman who will love me,
and not discard me because of my blindness;
I wanna drive and find a career;
I want sight to reel me in from the margins
of both society and darkness.
I don't wanna feel shame from not seeing,
for being misunderstood for my blind-
induced follies that trip me up daily.

Intoxication is like a pair of dark glasses
that I hide behind to cover my blindness.
It's easier to blame insobriety
for my stupid stunts than for me to admit
that most of the blame belongs to this phantom
that clings to me every day and every night,
an obstacle builder blighting my path.
He can't hurt me here inside my armor,
where I wield cans of *Budweiser* and weed.

And if you listen very hard

30

The tune will come to you at last
When all is one and one is all, yeah
To be a rock and not to roll.

And she's buying the stairway to heaven . . . .

* * *

Part Eight, The Move

Our time to depart from Lakeland arrived:
it was November 30, 1974.
And although the location of my life
on that Saturday was about to change,
other parts of it would remain the same:
"How many times have I told ya, Matt,
'Do NOT smoke in this house?'" Mom scolded.
"Uncle Sherman does," I argued. "And besides,
it's our last day here. So what's the difference?"

Stationed with an air of impatience,
the *U-Haul* sat idling on our street,
until dad thwarted its flow of fuel with the turn of a key.
He and Uncle Sherman then opened the container door
and pulled its ramp out onto the ground:
a 45 degree plank on which to transport our possessions.

"Go to war, Jack, be careful with my hutch.
Ya guys almost hit the top of the doorway!"
Mom squawked, supervising from the sidewalk.
"So, Mary, do ya wanna do it yourself?" Dad retorted.

Lakeland was like a loved one to me,
who was about to die, with a physician
prepared to pull the plug on its life support.
And just like how, when a person passed away,
people kept going on with their daily business,
so, too, the neighborhood continued to rotate
anesthetized on its axis—
the normal order of a Saturday interrupted only by
our *U-Haul* anchored in its harbor on Norland Road.
That ship, with its container stuffed with cargo, had
already departed three times for Pasadena

and had returned again—
this time to reload for its final voyage.

"I'm goin' for a bike ride, dad. I'll be back."
"Don't be long, Matt. I wanna be gone by dark."
I bicycled against a breeze that slapped
against my chilled cheeks. If a few degrees colder,
my tears might have frosted on my face.
I parked my bike at the top of the hill,
overlooking the park I played at for years.
After five matches I finally breathed life
into my *Salem,* while it stole mine.
Dusk slowly began robbing the sky of day,
yet light still ruled from lofty lamps
that hovered high above our city streets.
Still not a soul around, it was as if
only ghosts had come out for play: not a peep
except from seats of swings smacking each other,
and the clanging from their twisting chains,
both elbowed about by the whirling wind.
More action in the 'burbs of Pasadena
than in my beloved Lakeland tonight,
I mused, while, at the same time, studying
that ever-present ball glove, which drooped
sadly from the middle of my handlebars.
Since my life had become permanently like that season
between the World Series and Spring Training,
what use would I have for some moth-eaten ball glove?
Slinging it like a *Frisbee,*
I watched as it cartwheeled to a stop, out of season,
and so, there, I left it upon that brittle hill.

And, then, after riding to my house one last time,
I pedaled up the plank of the *U-Haul*
and parked my bike in the back of the truck.

Dad, meanwhile, closed the door,
as I took one last look around my street,
branding it onto my mind.
I watched my sister climb into the cab,
dragging behind her that old *Mrs. Beasley* doll,
carefully wrapped in a bedraggled blanket.

By the time we unpacked our *U-Haul*,
nighttime deepened in Pasadena.
As raindrops started pelting us,
like birdshot being tossed from the heavens,
I hurried to the house, clipping my hand
on the corner of a column that pillared
an awning on the face of our house.
I staggered, dazed in the darkness.
Dropping the box I carried, I squeezed my hand.
And after wringing the pain from it,
I put it in front of my face and saw nothing!
Was I the only one noticing how dark Pasadena was?
No one else certainly seemed bothered by it.

"Take your shoes off before ya come in here,"
mom commanded, as I walked through the front door.

As I settled into my bed that night,
the smell of fresh lumber reminded me
of Mr. Smith's woodshop class at my old school.
And, then, I thought about how
the *woods* in our old yard consisted of only three trees:
a plum, a maple, and a crabapple.
Each of which dwarfed in comparison
to the scores of oaks towering in our new yard,
that danced that night to the music of a storm,
performing like a concert in the nearby bay,
while gusts from its wind instruments sawed off limbs,

that bombarded our rooftop like missiles.
I worried not about the storm but about
beginning a new school in the middle of the year.

***

Part Nine, George Fox

On Monday, December 2, 1974,
my terror began as a new student
at George Fox Junior High.
And who the heck was George Fox, anyway?

I wanted to close the curtain on this day
long before the sunrise ever opened it.
But because our school day began at noon,
by the time I even started to head down the street
to catch the bus at its stop,
this Monday morning had already dragged on
like a midnight mass on Christmas Eve.
If only I had some pot to caulk the seams of my nerves.
Instead, I grappled with my panic
by chain-smoking seven straight cigarettes.

Meanwhile, as I lumbered toward the bus stop,
as if my feet had been manacled,
a guy approached me in a jean jacket
with a bandana, that, perhaps, might have been
tied a little too tight around his head.

"Hey, you moved into that new house up the street.
Didn't you?" He said.
"Yep."
"Yeah, I saw you Saturday in your yard. We were hoping,
since your house swallowed up a favorite partying trail,
for some foxes to move in to compensate for our losses.
Disappointed again, I see! You're Matt, right?"

"Yeah," I said. "How did ya know that?"
"I have to get my *Paradise Lost* book,"
he said, ignoring me.

"Ninth grade has to write a paper on it. Hey,
do you have an extra cigarette?"

I tossed him a *Salem*.
"What's this? Menthol? It'll have to do I guess,
until I get a pack of *Marlboros*.
I'm Nathan Carlyle, by the way.   See ya!"

You're welcome, moron. I thought to myself.
And ya never did answer my question!

Beyond the normal fears I fretted about
starting a new school at the midyear mark,
like making new friends, fitting in, and overcoming
the new-kid-on-the-block stigma,
anxiousness over what visual mishaps
that might await me became a pestilence,
circulating through the veins of my mind.
I kept telling myself over and over,
Just pay attention and you'll be all right.
Since seeing had become such a chore, though,
just paying attention
might not be a powerful enough lens for clarity.

Whatever ya do, I reminded myself,
*don't sit on anyone when ya get on
that bus and your eyes go into timeout mode,
like that time, on the 28 Lakeland Bus,
when ya unwittingly sat on the lap
of that elderly woman. And the guy
next to her, probably misinterpreting
your blunder as disrespect, hollered:*
*"What the heck's wrong with you, jerk? Didn't you
see her sitting there? Open your eyes next time!"*

I felt like I was back in right field again,

37

with the bases loaded, praying my old prayer:
Please don't let 'em hit the ball my way!
As the noon hour grew ever closer,
I jumped into the bus stop with both feet
like a swimmer who plunges into a pool
acclimating himself to the cold water.
A girl with dark, ratty hair balanced her butt
delicately on a cable festooned between two pilings,
both hands on a book that absorbed her face.

"Whaddya readin'?" I asked.
"Milton's *Paradise Lost*," she said,
her eyes still screwed to the pages.
"Who are you?" She asked.
"I'm Matt Harris, just moved in up the street."
"I'm Liz Knowles," she said, unfastening
her eyes from her book. "Your first day, huh?"
"Yep."
"That must suck! Gotta smoke?" She asked.

Does anyone around here have their own cigarettes?
I wondered to myself, promising
to stop being the neighborhood cigarette machine.
After lighting a *Salem* for her,
she gave her attention back to Milton.

The bus grumbled to a halt. And I followed
Liz up its steps, on passed the driver,
while my eyes went into *timeout* mode.
But since the bus wasn't too crowded,
I landed safely in an empty seat.
So far, so good. Just pay attention, Matt,
I reminded myself, as my eyes focused.
Liz lounged in the last seat of the bus, knees pressed
against the seat in front of her, head back

38

staring intently at the ceiling.
As the bus filled, while making its rounds,
I felt invisible, as more kids poured on.
I was grateful no one sat beside me.

The noontime sun reflected from the concrete
and pierced through my eyes like a sewing needle
stitching a tapestry of blinding light,
through which I maneuvered from the bus
to the entrance of George Fox Junior High School.
As I fell in line with a flow of kids,
despite my internal admonition to myself—

Pay attention. Don't run into anyone—

I still stepped on and bumped into people,
while *excuse me* seemed like the only words I knew.
On the one hand, I felt as if I stood out
like a lone tree surrounded by a vast field.
While at the same time, on the other hand,
I felt as if I were dead, like a ghost
that floated through the land of the living.

At last, I found *English 147.*
As I walked through the door, the bell sounded.
"Hi, I'm Matt Harris. This is my first day,"
I said to my first period teacher.
"Let me see," she said. "Yes.
There you are in my roll book. Nice to meet you.
My name is Mrs. Czyrwiezki. But call me Mrs. C.
Oh, here, take this book, *Paradise Lost,* by John Milton.
It's a poem the class is reading.
Are you familiar with the book, Matt?"
"No ma'am," I said.
"But I know Milton was blind when he wrote it."

"Yes," Mrs. C said. "That's right. Very good, Matt.
You can take a seat now,
right over there behind Gregory Kilmer.
He's that gentleman in the green jacket."

Green was as foreign as Greek to me;
but worse than that, Mrs. C must have pointed
to where Gregory Kilmer was seated. And, of course,
my peripheral vision did not detect her simple directions,
so I wandered off in the opposite way,
where that familiar sound—laughter—greeted me.

"You stoned or something, dude? Greg's over there,"
one of my classmates said, my central vision
picking up his finger pointing to where
that gentleman in the green jacket sat.
Slinking off to my desk, I opened up Milton,
wishing to lose myself inside *Paradise Lost.*

After the final bell rang at 5:30,
everyone flew through the doors in a frenzy.
Darkness had already spilled like ink
across the parking lot packed with buses and kids.
And though *whiteout,* at least, left my eyes alone,
blackness slowed my pace more than a little bit.
As I looked out across the parking lot from the sidewalk,
where I shuffled, searching for bus number *249,*
my shins were suddenly bludgeoned by impact.
It was like a soccer striker had struck them,
while attempting to steal the ball from me.
I tossed my binder like a hot potato
and braced myself with both hands to brake my fall,
as pain pounded from my ankles to my knees.
Laughter, that familiar foe, blasted me,
while kids walked by without any hands to help.

I stooped and groped along the ground to find
the place where my loose-leaf binder landed.
Later, I learned I had tripped into a large box,
filled with frozen earth,
designed not for an idiot like me to fall into
but rather for a large flower garden to bloom.

"Over here, Matt." Liz yelled from the bus,
apparently having witnessed my mishap.
And as if nothing had happened, I embarked
249 for the long ride home.

When we arrived at our stop, *whiteout,*
timeout, and poor peripheral vision
at that hour had become nonissues,
since darkness had trumped the trio.
I saw nothing except the shades of light
that flickered from porch lamps.
I walked home with my left foot on the shoulder,
and my right foot on the road,
wondering how I'd ever find my house,
until I saw a glimpse of dad's Ford parked in our yard,
painted with light that was brushed by the beams
illuminating from the lamp in our yard.
I felt for my keys and opened the front door,
engulfed by Irish Stew's homespun smell;
its spices mingled with mom's command:
"Go to war, Matt! Take your shoes off, will ya?"

* * *

Part Ten, Old Grand-Dad

Yanking Zeppelin from its 8-track chamber,
I bash the dash again, tuning in the game,
as Eddie Murray rounds the bases,
after belting a solo blast to tie the score at 2
in the top of the fourth inning.

I should probably sell my Mustang
before it falls apart and won't be worth a dime bag.

"Claws, what the heck ya sneakin' up on me for?
Ya scared the crap right out of me, man."
"I'm not sneakin'. I'm just peekin' at this rust
that's eatin' away at your quarter panel," Claws says,
while sipping some *Old Grand-Dad.*
"When ya puttin' her back on the road, Matt?"
"When I get the money, I guess," I lied.
"Ya already work fulltime, dude.
Ya need to find a new job makin' more money,
before this beauty wastes away for good."

Claws' real name is Brian Crabtree,
but everybody always calls him Claws.
He likes whiskey, particularly *Old Grand-Dad.*
That habit began in tenth grade,
after a flame felled a local store called *Angels.*
When the ashes and brimstone settled,
Claws and I paid a visit to dear *Old Grand-Dad,*
salvaging some cases from the shelves of fallen *Angels.*

We hauled a load of spirits in our arms,
while hurrying like pack mules across the parking lot.
Claws spotted a cop in his squad car on patrol—
probably on the lookout for looters!

We took cover inside a patch of tall weeds,
as the cop shined his light on the parking lot,
barely denting the darkness surrounding us.
Breathing not a breath until the law left,
Claws and I were drunk on adrenalin,
and for months afterward drunk on *Old Grand-Dad.*

I had learned by then to maneuver better at night
by listening to my friends' footsteps
and following the sounds of their movements.
And though I memorized the trails we passed through,
many times I still would walk into trees,
or trip on an unanticipated bump.

"Who's winnin'?" Claws asks.
"It's tied at 2," I say.
"Wanna go see who's hangin' out down The Park?"
"Nah. Maybe I'll catch up with ya later, Claws.
I'm gonna finish listenin' to the game."

Claws always knew something was amiss about my sight.
But whenever that troublesome issue arose,
I would always abruptly change the subject.
One time he advised me to look down at the ground
more often when I walked at night.
He wasn't being a smart aleck, though.
He was really trying to help me out.

"John Lowenstein fouls off Mark Langford's fastball.
And the count is even: one ball, one strike,"
Chuck Thompson says, calling the game from his booth.
"Lowenstein's batting two forty-nine this year
and struck out in his first at bat today.
Langford throws a low outside breaking ball,
and Lowenstein hits a slow roller

toward Shooty Babitt, the second baseman,
who tosses it over to Jim Spencer at first
for the final out of the inning,"
Thompson bellows, before sending us off
to listen to more stupid commercials,
putting me asleep for awhile until . . .

"Hey, Matt, wake up. Ya alright?" Jenny Young asks,
her fist banging on my driver's-side roof.
"Yeah. I just nodded off a bit. What's up?"
"I'm gettin' some stuff for mom at the store.
Ya wanna walk up with me?" She asks.
"Nah. I just wanna stay here and catch a buzz."
"Looks like you're already buzzed. Somethin' wrong?"
"Just thinkin' about some things, that's all."
"It looked like ya wuz snoozin' more than thinkin',"
Jenny chuckles, then reminiscing, says,
"Hey! Remember when *you* used to shop for mom?
She'd give ya a store list. You'd steal the crap
and only charge her half price for the stuff.
Mom always loves gettin' a good bargain."
"Yeah, of course, I remember. I'm not senile."
"Keep smokin' that wacky weed and ya will be."
"Ya smoke it way more than I do, girl."
"Yeah, but I have more brain cells to burn than you."
Jenny needles, while heading off to the store.
"Hey. Bring me back some *Doritos,*" I yell.

Jenny and I have been close friends for years.
And though I'm clueless about her eye color,
I still love the way they flicker when she laughs.
And all of us guys around here agree:
she fills out her *Levis* rather nicely.
But what I like best about her is this:
we can talk effortlessly for hours.

And, yet, as easily as we converse,
I still can't share with her my ordeal.

* * *

Part Eleven, Angel Dust

During the first few months at my new school,
ninth grade moved along at a pace not unlike
how a lazy man might prepare for work.
While the feet of winter trudged through its season,
even in February I liked our beach. There,
peace always massaged my shoulders whenever I heard
the sound of the creek slapping the shoreline.
The locals referred to the beach as *The Park*;
and since now I was a bona fide *local,*
I began to call the beach The Park, too.

I had met a few people by then, but still
I felt all alone as if I didn't exist.
Liz Knowles introduced me to Ralphie Nelson—
our neighborhood drug dealer.
Ralphie drove a light-colored Toyota Corolla,
didn't work, didn't go to school, just sold drugs.
Whenever his Corolla cruised by The Park,
it conjured up in my mind the snowball truck
that once rumbled through the streets of Lakeland.
In contrast to that little kid I once was,
who thirsted for strawberry snowballs
with a mountain of marshmallow piled on top,
I now hungered with other teenagers for a nickel
or a dime bag of weed, or a hearty hunk of hash.
And unlike how we used to have to holler *wait a minute*
to halt the snowball truck as we chased it down the street,
Ralphie's Corolla required no such pleading for it to stop,
because he slammed on its brakes every time he saw us,
to earn his ill-gotten gain by feeding our dependencies,
exploiting that abyss which existed in each of our souls.

Darkness was just about to cast its net,

as I approached the driver's-side window.
"What goodies ya got today, Ralphie?" I asked.
"Ya seen Nathan?" Ralphie asked.
"No." I said.
"Let's ride. We're wasting heat." Ralphie said,
turning up "Smoke on the Water" full throttle.

As soon as I shut the passenger's-side door,
he lit a joint, inhaled, and passed it my way.
Exhaling into a creaking cough,
he snorted and shouted, "Red Mexican!"
His hacking betrayed the harshness of his weed.
Still, I took a hit, but not too deeply.
"A bit coarse," I said.
His throaty laugh clashed with his sales pitch:
"After a few hits it'll taste as smooth as a *Marlboro*."
"This crap will turn your lungs inside out," I laughed.

After another hit, I passed it back,
hoping to finish the darn thing before nightfall,
since it challenged me to try and find joints and bowls
whenever someone tried handing them to me in the dark.
I'd follow the glow cast forth from the joint or bowl,
yet oftentimes I'd lose them in the darkness still.
Usually when I missed them,
I just blamed it on the buzz. Yet it created angst for me,
and question marks I'm sure in people's minds arose.

"Grab that *roach clip* in the glove box," Ralphie said.
"We can get a couple more hits from this."

About a quarter inch of the joint remained;
at that length it was referred to as a roach.
Roach clips were like tweezers that hooked onto it:
a useful tool to keep people's fingers away from the heat.

While smokers held its handle and toked on the roach,
only they, instead of the weed, got wasted.

When we stopped back at The Park,
Ralphie snatched Deep Purple from his 8-track player.
Always fearing I'd get busted riding around with Ralphie,
I was grateful for another safe return—un-arrested.
Then pulling ten bucks from my pocket,
I bought a dime bag of Ralphie's *Red Mexican.*
My sense of touch told me it was a good count;
and my sense of smell told me it was pot;
and that was really all I needed to know.
Before I could put the baggie away,
someone banged on my window and yelled, "Busted!"

"Nathan, ya must have mush for brains," Ralphie roared,
as I rolled down my window and saw blackness.
"I ought to whoop up on ya," he added.
"Open up, burnout! It's cold," Nathan ordered,
before squeezing into the backseat.

Nathan Carlyle went to the same church
my mom, my sister, and I attended: St. Jane Francis—
another *fine* Catholic boy just like me.
But our similarities ended there.
He concealed a Judas-like spirit, which betrayed him
every time someone would leave his presence.
Arrows from his quiver of insults flew at their backs.
I often chuckled to myself at those who laughed
at the barbs Nathan blasted at people behind their backs,
since they became his bull's-eyes after they left as well.

"I finally found some flakes for you, Ralphie,"
Nathan bragged, while loading up a bowl.
"It took ya long enough," Ralphie chided.

"Oh! And, by the way, moron, I didn't mean
Frosted Flakes," Ralphie teased.
"And I hope Tony the Tiger didn't bite ya," I added,
as Ralphie roared: *"They're Grrrrreat!"*

When Nathan smacked me hard in the head,
I turned toward the darkness and warned,
"Touch me again, Nathan, and I'll bash ya."
"If you're gonna whoop up on him, Matt,
just don't bloody up my car," Ralphie chuckled.
"I gotta go find me a tree to water," he added.

After Ralphie bolted through the door,
Nathan said to me,
"I wish he'd take a bath sometimes.
He always smells like a litter box.
You know what I mean, Matt?"
"Not really," I lied.

Flakes were parsley treated with a drug
called Phencyclidine or PCP,
also known on the street as *Angel Dust.*
This dust, however, did not descend
from any angelic host from heaven, though;
but rather it ascended from the fallen ones,
imprisoned in the chambers of Hades.
But regardless of its origins,
it was a hallucinogenic that rocketed
my friends and me to other universes!

After Ralphie had returned from his mission,
the flake bowl made its rounds throughout the night
in a triangular fashion: from Nathan,
sitting in the middle of the backseat,
to Ralphie, stationed behind the wheel,

49

then to me, seated in the front passenger's seat.
When a sizzling sound started inside my ears,
like bacon frying in a skillet,
I knew this crackling was internal, because
Ralphie blasted Black Sabbath full volume,
blocking out all noise but Ozzy Osbourne.

Were these lost souls hissing in hell? I wondered.

While a shudder seized each shoulder,
I became spellbound
by what seemed like a demon shoveling
a grave with a corrupt spade in the basement
of my psyche. I saw an iron gate,
not upright but lying on the ground,
and not a single pearl decorating it,
night inhaling me inside Ralphie's Corolla
like the great fish that once swallowed Jonah.
While blinded inside the theater of Night,
I watched a spiritual horror flick
projected on the screen of my mind.

Was that Cerberus' bark, that hellish hound
with his three heads, guarding Hades' door?

My turn came to draw from the pipe again,
as I watched the parsley flakes twinkle like stars.
Ralphie started up the Corolla and yelled,
"Let it ride!"
As his tires squealed and fishtailed
on the frigid February road,
it was as if we had become detached,
like little children participating in parallel play,
each of us engaged in our own unique hallucination
with the bowl of flakes as our primary toy.

Ralphie's driving seemed so precise,
as if the Corolla glided along like a monorail.
The lights from oncoming traffic appeared
as if they were about to jump in our lane,
and we wouldn't have felt the pain if they had.
We were on a magic carpet ride, indeed!
Every time the last flake flickered out,
Nathan topped off the bowl with another batch—
like an attentive barkeep filling a glass
with spirits as soon as someone emptied it.
The more I smoked the more I sank
into a dimension beyond the physical realm,
conjuring up influences from domains
that breached my borders and trespassed through my soul.

When Ralphie stopped back at The Park again,
I opened the car door, wordless, and stepped out
into the cold air that warmed me with relief.
My feet felt bare through my *Easy Walker* shoes,
thinking for some reason they'd been sliced open.
When I touched them, though, they were perfectly intact,
while numbness permeated my body,
not from the cold but from some foreign entity.
As I wandered home from The Park,
I treaded gingerly on the double-yellow lines,
when I spotted them from collateral light,
amid the barren road that led back home.
And like how poets use lines in their poems
to pilot their craft toward epiphany,
the double-yellows likewise captained me
through the haze to the unveiling of my house.
While fear that the street might sever my feet
slashed through my thinking like a razorblade,
I hallucinated that I had fallen
straight down through the earth,

until I landed between the double-yellows,
while inching onward toward my goal,
with that ceaseless sound of bacon sizzling,
its hellish grease splattering inside my head,
until I entered my deserted house,
then dreamt while wide awake until the dawn.

***

Part Twelve, The Next Day

"Matt, it's noon. Ya gonna sleep all day?" Mom yelled,
striking the side of my bed with her broom.
"Go help dad with the paneling in his den."

It was like I'd awakened from delusion
and still was unable to discern the parts
that were fact from the ones which were fiction.
While confusion from PCP daunted my demeanor,
the smell of bacon drove me to the kitchen,
its sizzle jerking me back again to last night.

"Hey Face," I greeted my sister, as she flipped
the bacon bathing in a frying pan filled with grease.
"Shut up!
Mom, Matt's calling me names again."

For no reason, other than to torment her,
I often referred to my sister as Face.
She hated when I dragged the "f" sound out:
"Fa-Fa-Fa-Face stop your tattlin'," I taunted.
"Leave your sister alone," mom bellowed
from her bedroom down at the end of the hall.
"Bye Fa-Fa-Fa-Face" I teased again, swiping
some slices of bacon that cooled on a plate.

"How's the den comin' along, dad?" I asked.
"I gotta go to the hardware store for nails.
Do ya wanna ride up there with me?"
"Sure. I need to buy some smokes, anyway."

While getting into my dad's Ford Galaxie,
I heard Ralphie and his dad, Ralph, Sr., start to laugh,
as they stood in their front yard,

neither having responded to my wave.
That's odd, I thought, as dad sped away.

"I invited Mr. Ralph to church," dad said.

Oh great, I thought, *that probably explains why
they were laughing and had ignored me*.

A couple of weeks after we had moved here,
dad started attending Lake Shore Baptist Church,
right up the street about a mile from our house.
Dad changed soon after he first sat on their pew,
from a man who rarely ever spoke of God
to a man who could not shut up about Him.

"So what did Mr. Ralph tell ya?" I asked.
"He said he didn't believe in fairytales,"
dad answered in a lamentable tone.

*Dang! Ain't it hard enough for me to fit in
around here*, I thought, *without my father
tellin' the whole neighborhood about Jesus?*

"For God so loved the world that he gave
his only begotten Son, that whosoever
believeth in him should not perish,
but have everlasting life," dad quoted from Scripture.

"God doesn't want anyone in hell,
tormented by its flames forever.
But it's your sin and mine, Matt, that put us there.
That's why He sent Jesus, His Son, to die
on the cross to forgive us of our sins.
It's God's gift to us, the greatest gift ever.
And all we have to do is receive it,

54

by grace through faith, by repenting from our sin,
and by believing in the Lord Jesus Christ."
Dad finished his piece, as we pulled
into the local hardware store called Aunt Sarah's.

"Why don't ya come to church with me tomorrow?"
Dad asked, almost pleading.

"Okay," I said.

I don't know why I agreed so easily.
Maybe after what I learned last night
from PCP, I needed a dose of church.

The next day, as we arrived at the service,
everyone was leaving. Church had ended.
"Crap! We forget to set the clocks ahead
for daylight savings time last night," I said.
"Yep, you're right. I'm so used to settin' them
ahead in the spring that I forgot this year
daylight savings time was in February," dad said.
"Well, ya can go to church with me next week, then."

* * *

Part Thirteen, High in My Mustang

I should probably put a *For Sale* sign
on my Mustang's window. But how can I?
It would be like selling my best friend.
I could get at least a thousand for it. But
it's not about the money. It's about hope,
hope that maybe one day I'll drive her again.

"After walking Ricky Henderson
and Dwayne Murphy in the sixth inning,
Earl Weaver has seen enough," Thompson says.
"He's replacing Palmer with Sammy Stewart.
The score remains tied at 2 runs apiece,
and we'll be right back after a word
from our sponsor," Thompson blasts from his booth.

"It's about time ya got back from the store.
What, did ya get lost or somethin'?" I joke,
as Jenny sinks into my bucket seat.
"Here! Take your *Doritos*. Why do ya do *that*?"
She demands.
"Whaddya mean?" I ask.
"When I hand ya stuff, ya rarely respond."
"I don't always pay attention, I guess."
"Well, pay attention! It annoys the crap out of me."
She squawks.
"Here. Load up the bong. Will ya?" I say,
while handing over the paraphernalia.

After Jenny fills the six chambers with weed,
she grabs the *Bic* from my shirt pocket,
then lights one up and then another.
"That's good stuff," she says, coughing through her nose,
her smile returning to her sweaty face.

"Ya look like ya feel better, now," I say.
"Here," she says, handing the bong back to me.
When I take it from her hand, I say,
"See, I'm payin' attention this time."
As she giggles she grabs us both
a beer from my cooler.

As I choke down two more hits from the bong,
Jenny silences the O's game and slips
some Eagles to nest in the 8-track player.
Reclining back in the seat a bit to rest,
she twists up the volume to
"Life in the Fast Lane."
And I am reminded of the time I wrecked my '66
Ford Fairlane on Thanksgiving Day 1977.

Oh boy! Angels were emptying out their buckets
of mop water on Pasadena that day.
And with broken windshield wipers,
I was stuck like a lunatic in bedlam, until
my best friend, *Budweiser*, and I solved the problem
by attaching a piece of string to each wiper blade.
After running the string through both
the driver's-side and passenger's-side windows,
I remember how satisfaction filled me,
while I drove and powered the wipers
with this contraption of twine with my right hand,
as I steered with my left hand, resting
my right hand only long enough to grab
and to gulp the *Budweiser* by my side.

When I turned onto Hickory Point Road,
I plugged in a favorite driving song,
"Let it Ride," by Bachman-Turner Overdrive.
I gave the engine a little extra juice,

then barely noticed a car backing out of its driveway.
Like a drummer pumping the pedal of the bass,
I pumped my brakes,
 as I slammed passenger's-side first into a tree.
A lady then asked me if I was okay.
All I could say was "Have I killed anyone?"
"No, hun. The only thing you hit was this old tree."
I felt instantly sobered and much relieved.

Within minutes I learned that the car
that had been backing out of the driveway
belonged to the daughter of the pastor
at my father's church: Lake Shore Baptist.
The cop who arrived at the scene knew me well,
since he had already busted me before—
on a larceny charge for stealing a bike.
I think the pastor somehow persuaded
the policeman not to arrest me,
and I was fortunate because I was still
on probation from my last arrest.

Shortly after moving to Pasadena,
I started stealing bikes, and whatever else
I thought I could acquire through thievery.
One Sunday, at age 17, I walked to the store
for the sole purpose of buying cigarettes—
not to steal anything.
But when I arrived and saw a kid park
his ten-speed bicycle in front of the store,
temptation called out to me, saying:
You can get forty bucks for that one. Take it!

Within minutes after I snatched it,
and hid it in the woods,
a cop walked into my backyard and arrested me.

After showing him where I ditched the bike,
he cuffed me and placed me in his cruiser,
while Mr. Ralph, the neighbor who kept
refusing my dad's invitation to church,
seemed to smirk as he witnessed a rebellious son
bring disgrace to his Godly father.
At least Mr. Ralph went to church *that* day,
even if it was only to find my father and gloat
while he told him how a cop took me away in handcuffs.

"Why aren't ya workin' today?" Jenny prods,
jerking me away from my foul memories.
"I felt like partyin', so I took off."
"Liar!" She squawks. "How can ya stand workin'
in that sweatshop with your ex's father?
Are ya masochistic or somethin', Matt?"
"Ya don't know what *masochistic* means, girl.
When did *you* start speakin' in ten-dollar words?"
"Shut up and answer me this, moron.
Do ya still see her there?"
"Every day," I say.
"Ya still love her. I know ya do," she says.
"I gotta get this crap home to mom,
before she sends a search party out for me.
Thanks for the buzz. And the *Doritos* are on me."
"Yeah. Well, ya better wipe 'em off ya," I slur.
"Ya don't wanna mess up those *Levi's*, girl!"
"Oh! So now you're a comedian, huh?
Very funny," she says,
"Don't quit your day job. No!
I take that back. Ya need to quit *that* job!"
Why did she have to bring *her* up?
Isn't RP enough to deal with today,
without thinking about Janie Graber?

* * *

59

Part Fourteen, Let's Fight

In the middle of the eleventh grade, I started
my fourth new school in just over 2 ½ years.
Only this time, I wasn't the only one changing schools.
Our whole class was moving into a brand new one
called Chesapeake Senior High.
By then, Pasadena perfectly suited me,
like a well-worn flannel shirt.
As I settled into its drug culture,
and relaxed pace, school became a place
where I'd only appear at every so often.
On most visits, I was drunk, or stoned, or both,
yet my *blindness* still besieged these walls
of insobriety I hid behind,
while it knocked the mortar from them bit by bit.

Before one such visit to school,
I'd lost count of how many shots of *Old Grand-Dad*
I had chugged with my friend, Jason Black.
Boozing, by then, had become a sport.
And like how a riding crop propels a horse along,
so, too, pride prodded my friends and me onward,
as we tried to outduel each other drinking.
Unfortunately, for me, and for those around me,
more times than not, drinking
reduced me to a quick-tempered lunatic.
And whatever thought popped into my head,
somehow it got vomited out of my mouth.
And such was the case when Jason drove us to school
that morning. We arrived late.
After entering my fourth period math class,
I dropped my head to the desk for a snooze.
Mrs. Morehead summed up her displeasure,
when she banged her fist on my desk and said,

"No one, Mr. Harris, sleeps in my class."
Her condescending tone triggered these words:
"Here's the common denominator!
If ya weren't so borin', Mrs. Morehead,
no one would be noddin' off in your class."

Amid the oohs and the ahs and the laughter from the class,
Mrs. Morehead threw my butt out.
As I sat in the administrator's office,
she kept asking me if I'd been drinking.
"No, I swear," I said every time she asked.
And though the grape bubble gum I gnawed on
helped to mask the alcohol on my breath a bit,
I was certain my eyes betrayed my lie,
because they turned a deep red whenever I partied
I was told. Because the administrator didn't know
exactly what to do with me,
she sent me home in a taxi cab.

Later that afternoon, at The Park,
I met up with Auggie Bell, and said,
"I heard Sonny Roberts hit on your gal, Annie."
"Yeah, and it's not the first time, either.
I'm gonna whoop up on him, Matt.
We're supposed to get it straight right here at 4:00.
Ya wanna back me up?
Nathan Carlyle promised to pitch in, too,
but as usual he'll probably be late."
"Why not," I volunteered,
"I ain't been in a brawl in a while."

I'd soon regret my decision. Sure enough,
right at 4:00,
Sonny and his friend, Donny Shores, swaggered up to us,
as Auggie greeted them,

"Hey, look, Matt, it's Sonny and Cher.
Why don't ya sing 'I Got You Babe' to each other?"

With that, Sonny shoved Auggie,
then fists flew between the two,
while Donny and I stood there staring at each other.
Suddenly I didn't want to be there.
But before I could decide what to do,
Donny broke the silence and said to me,
"What's your problem, moron?"
"I take care of my problems. What's yours, sea Shores,"
I barbed.

I don't know if I would have seen it or not,
even if I would have had perfect vision.
But after his right fist crashed into my nose,
and although my knees buckled a bit,
we both were surprised I was still standing.
My nose bled like a ketchup bottle
in a glutton's hand at a French-fry feast.
While white specks floated in front of my eyes,
like tiny insects fluttering about,

Don't let him hit ya again, I warned myself.

If he did, I knew he'd knock my butt out.
The battle seemed to slow. It became distant.
Dad always told me, *if ya fight, fight to win.*
So I used my feet to keep my head from the fray.
I kicked him in the torso and the knees,
though I was aiming for his groin.
After landing several promising punches,
I got him in a headlock and bled all over his back,
while Sonny and Auggie stood in the street, watching us
like a couple of spectators at Madison Square Garden.

After what seemed like an eternity,
Donny and I called it quits for the day.
And when everyone left, I sat on the ground,
weary and woozy, holding my head back,
trying to stop my nose from bleeding.

Several weeks later, as I worked my shift
at the Royal Farm Store, I wondered how long
it would take for customers to ask me,
after I had already rung them up,
Did you get the Coke, or the gum, or the chips?
The honest ones were being helpful, I knew.
But it was still embarrassing to miss ringing up
items that sat in plain view right in front of me.
Sure, I would see some of them but not all.
The more incompetent I felt,
the more numb I became to the world around me.

By then, I'd been working at the store
for months as a cashier and a stock boy.
But I enlarged the borders of my billfold
by practicing the art of embezzlement.
As I grew older, a mindset developed,
like a vine twisting around my thinking,
that I was entitled to take what I pleased.
And to everyone else in society,
catch me if ya can was my challenge to them.
As the night wore on, Janie Graber,
and one of her friends, dropped in to buy some stuff.
Janie lived right down the street from the store.
And on her frequent visits,
we flirted and exchanged pleasantries.

"Did you get the *Mound's Bar*, Matt?" Janie asked,
after I'd already rung up her soda and smokes,

but oblivious to her candy bar,
sitting in plain view right next to her soda can.
"No. I forgot, sorry," I said sheepishly.
"No need to be sorry," she cooed in a way
that seemed to make everything all right.

And even my bad eyes could see how she moved
her body with great deftness toward the front door.
I knew it was probably wishful thinking
even to consider her visits might in some way
be ostensible for her to come in and talk with me.

Erase those thoughts from your head right now, ya jerk,
I ordered myself. *She's trouble. After all,*
she's had a boyfriend for several years. And besides,
she's not just friendly with you but with everyone else, too.

And yet how was I able to resist
the way she carried her scrawniness,
or batted those puppy dog eyes at me,
or that wisp of stray, dark hair that more often
than not danced on her cheek below her left eye,
or her sweet words, as they poured out
through a smile revealing a slight overbite,
that punctuated her face with uniqueness?
No weapons of war could have withstood that battle!
It was as if she was the sea's bottom,
and someone tied cinder blocks to my legs
and hurled me into the ocean's depths.

The next day, as I stood in our school's smoking area,
Janie grabbed my arm and said, "Hey, Matt,
give me a light. You forgot to give me matches yesterday,
when I bought my smokes. I'm going to tell your boss!"
"You're gonna get me fired, girl. And then

who's gonna only charge ya for a small coffee
when ya buy a large one?" I reminded her.
"Then just don't let it happen again, mister,"
she smiled while sauntering down the walkway.

Not long after my brawl with Donny Shores,
we gained mutual respect for each other,
and became friends and ate lunch together,
whenever I paid a visit to school.
And on those occasions, Janie Graber
and her friend, Katie Latzman, also joined us.
During lunchtime one day, while we laughed,
flirted and kidded around, as we chowed down
our pork 'n' beans and cold cut submarines,
a substance splattered on the side of my face.
I heard laughter from the table beside us,
as I wiped off the glob of mayonnaise from my cheek.
Jocks, showing off for Katie and Janie, had hit their mark.
And I hit mine,
after catapulting a spoonful of beans amid their huddle.
Janie choked on her milk, as she laughed mid-gulp,
while Donny looked at me and said, "Uh-oh!"
Katie excused herself for the ladies' room.
Jocks at our school hated long-haired potheads like me,
who wore sleeveless jean jackets with phrases
of self-expression etched ever so poetically
on our backs like the one emblazoned on mine:
Born to be Wild.
Tit for tat, and that was that, I thought.

After having arrived at the smoking area,
I lit my cigarette and leaned against
the outside glass to the cafeteria.
"Why did you hit me with pork 'n' beans, punk?"
Craig Myerson asked, as I blew smoke

from my *Salem* in his face, and said,
"Someone threw mayo in my face first, jock strap!"

What would prognosticators predict
if a two-hundred-pound linebacker type punched
a one-hundred-forty-pound warrior poet?
Extreme pain? Lots of blood? Probably.
But this time their prophecy would be false.

When Myerson planted his first punch,
just below my left eye,
it sat me on the cement for a second.
As I cleared my head, and mustered courage,
I sprang to my feet, while Myerson just laughed
and belted me in the forehead. Undaunted,
I felt nothing but adrenaline-fueled fury,
as I peppered him with punches to the face and body.
I was quick enough not to let the oaf grab me.
I did not want this to turn into a wrestling match.

"What are ya doin'? Get off me!" I hollered,
as two teachers collared me from behind.
As Myerson lunged toward me, I jumped up
and kicked him in the throat, freeing myself
from my captors. I pursued my predator again,
when suddenly I tasted concrete,
as Mr. Jensen, our gym teacher,
grappled me to the ground from behind.
Our bout earned us both a five-day vacation;
and after my suspension ended,
I returned to school and received some sound advice
from a kid I didn't even know who stopped me in the hall:
"The next time you get into a fight," he said,
"Why not pick on someone your own size?"

* * *

Part Fifteen, Comfortably Numb

Why can't I get my butt outta this Mustang?
It's not like it's fastened to the seat,
more like my motivation has been bled out,
staining the carpet of my ambition.
I have no desire to deal with blindness;
it's like a belt that binds my inner being,
strangling the energy that tries to escape.
What shall I do? I am already losing
my ability to function at work.
I've fractured my left hand twice in six months,
while punching out bolt holes in asbestos
gaskets with a hammer and a punch.
Our bosses say the asbestos won't hurt us,
since it's *compressed*. But what about when we cut it
and its dust flutters in the air like falling snow?
I can look forward to white lung, I suppose.
At least it takes decades for it to surface.
Janie Graber, maybe I still do love ya,
even though ya belong to another now.
I'll let *Budweiser* take that pain away,
even if it is just for a moment.

"We're in the top half of the eighth,
still tied at 2, with Rick Dempsey at bat,
while Rich Dauer awaits in the on-deck circle,"
Chuck Thompson voices through the AM static.
"Dempsey takes ball one from Rick Langford,
who's fanned eight batters so far," Thompson adds.
"Dempsey lines one into right-center field
for a base hit, his second of the day."

Come on Dauer get a hold of one.
Let's put this game away already!

"Do ya like talkin' to yourself, Matt?
Ya know what? You're the easiest person
in all of Pasadena to sneak up on," Jenny says,
standing next to my driver's-side window.

"Oh, there they are," she says,
reaching across me to grab her cigarettes from my console.
"I just bought some hash from Tony Gleason.
Ya wanna smoke some?" She asks.
"Or am I interruptin' your stupid baseball game?"

Before I have a chance to answer,
she marches in front of my car,
while en route to my passenger's-side seat,
which absorbs her butt she's always complaining is fat.
She makes herself at home,
replacing the ballgame with Pink Floyd.
She loads her bowl with blond hash and fires it up,
her face contorting from a croup-like cough,
while expelling smoke. She passes it my way.

Four years ago, Tony Gleason and I
stole his mother's Volkswagen one evening,
neither of us having had a license yet.
After hours of drinking and riding around,
Tony slammed dead center into an oak tree on a trail
in the woods where everyone liked to party.
My head knocked the windshield onto the hood,
while my knees dented the glove compartment.
I suffered cuts, bruises, and a concussion,
and the steering wheel knocked some of Tony's teeth out.

Fortunately, his mother did not press charges.
And since I was on probation, it kept me out of jail.
That was the first of eight car accidents

I'd participate in during a two-year span:
Four involved my own cars, and four
I was with friends while they wrecked theirs.
Blindness and intoxication don't mix well.

"Hey, Jenny, this hash is just what the doctor ordered.
I have become *comfortably numb.*"

* * *

Part Sixteen, Driving Blind

On the first day of my senior year,
I drove my white Ford Fairlane to school.
It was a *beater* but was paid for in full
from the funds I'd saved from working and thieving.
Though I failed many tests I should have passed,
the one I should have failed I passed:
my eye test at the MVA for my driver's license.
For months, prior to passing my driver's test,
percussion from two questions kept resounding
over and over again in my mind, while worries
sandwiched themselves between their impact:
Could I even see well enough *to* drive?
And if not, wouldn't the MVA find out?

Since it was every young man's dream to drive,
I pursued my goal with tunnel vision,
both literally and figuratively.
I failed the first test without ever realizing
I had sped through the stoplight.

"Pull over and put the vehicle in park, son,"
the driving instructor commanded.

After a month of beating myself up,
for either being too stupid or too blind—
I didn't know which to blame for my failure—
I advanced a little further through the course,
during my second test,
until I backed into a wall attempting a three-point turn,
as I heard my instructor blast these words again:

Put the vehicle in park, son.

After my third attempt at the test,

the course already etched in my memory,
I received my driver's license,
and of course,
without any restrictions at all for my eyes.
That meant my *blindness* was all in my head. Right?
Maryland wouldn't issue a license to a kid
with poor eyesight. Would they?

My driver's license only addled my brain,
as more doubts about my sanity surfaced. Still,
I rarely drove at night. And when I did,
I steered away from unfamiliar roads,
never straying from streets with double-yellow lines,
which I used as a guide to keep my train on track.
Even during the day,
I bridled my Mustang to gallop on a course
foddered with double-yellows and well-known routes.

I knew that under no circumstance should I ever
even remotely consider driving through
the Baltimore Harbor Tunnel.
When I'd ridden as a passenger through it,
my eyes would instantly enter *timeout* mode.
And they'd only readjust to it
when we were about to exit the channel,
1 ½ miles later, just in time
for my eyes to enter their *whiteout* phase,
as we resurfaced from the tunnel into daylight.

Midway through the first semester of twelfth grade,
I partied just about every day.
While sipping *Old Grand-Dad,* gulping *Budweisers,*
and smoking weed and PCP, my descent
into the pit of self-extinction quickened.
By Halloween, I was failing every course;

and since I needed to pass all my classes
to graduate in 1978,
I went AWOL from Chesapeake High School.
And, so, like a cook who slings hash on a grill,
I slung my education on the scrap heap.

By Christmas, I had mustered enough courage
to ask Janie Graber out for a date.
And to my surprise, she said, "Of course."
Janie Graber was not in my league at all;
besides her beauty, she was smart and rich.
Her father owned a machine shop and lavished
Janie with a comfortable lifestyle.
I would have loved to have taken her out
to a movie or to dinner alone in my own car.
But since my driving skills proved unsteady,
even when I was sober,
I needed to devise a plan quickly,
that did not include me behind the wheel.
My *blindness* was NOT going to mess this up.

That evening I called my old friend
from Lakeland, Jeeter Jones, and set up
a double date with him and Janie's friend,
Katie Latzman, along with Janie and me.
On Saturday evening, we picked up the girls
in Jeeter's Ford Pinto at Janie's house.
Against my argument to the contrary,
Jeeter brought along a quarter pound of weed
to sell and to smoke. The girls wanted to see
Saturday Night Fever,
but by the time we arrived at the theater,
we decided instead to keep stoking our buzzes,
heightened already by the falling snow,
which added to the remains of a storm
that had pummeled Pasadena days before.

As soon as we entered Fort Smallwood Park—
a stronghold the U.S. once used to protect
the entrance to The Baltimore Harbor
but by 1977 had become a popular hangout for partiers—
an unplowed trail became an overnight stall
for the Pinto as its hooves spun helplessly.

"Jeeter, where did ya learn to drive, ya moron?"
I scolded, as he mercifully replaced
The Bee Gees with The Who.
Luckily, we had just restocked the Pinto
with beer and burgers from McDonalds.

"Jeeter, where's your common sense?
If the cops come and find that weed,
I told ya *not* to bring, we're all gonna get busted.
And I'm still . . ."

Janie interrupted me with a tug on my jacket sleeve,
as if to say *let it go,*
and then stole a hearty bite from my burger.
"Bon Appetite, ya Hamburglar," I said.
What a dull-witted thing to say, I thought.
Even though sincerity laced her giggle,
I wished I could had seen her face right then.

As Jeeter lost himself in "Teenage Wasteland,"
Katie became as nippy toward him
as the brittle breeze shaking our Pinto,
that blew from across the Patapsco River.
At least the Pinto's heater worked well,
keeping us toasty inside our metal ice box
throughout the night. Janie and I talked
easily about our lives and dreams.
One of her goals was to become Honored Queen

in an organization called Job's Daughters,
which was connected with the masons somehow.
What a classy girl I remembered thinking,
so different from other girls I'd dated.
Janie slept with her head on my shoulder, till
the sun rose and a fellow with a snowplow
helped scoop us out of our predicament.
When we took Janie home her father was
wide-eyed and waiting in the driveway.
He did not believe for one minute
that we were marooned in a snowdrift all night.
And though Janie's father wanted to choke me
for keeping his daughter out all that night,
weeks later he still offered me a job,
after Janie highly recommended me,
to work at his machine shop in Baltimore.

One of my tasks at Graber's Machine Shop was
to unload trucks when materials arrived.
Physically, this was not a problem for me;
but visually, I was presented with a challenge.
Whenever I went from inside to outside and vice versa,
timeout and *whiteout,* of course, hindered my movement.
While these obstacles ping ponged back and forth,
and with diminished peripheral vision,
I unloaded these trucks as if I were blind,
which created a great deal of stress for me,
a pain in which I endured alone.
Even though Janie and I had become close,
I never shared my *blindness* with her.
How could I? I didn't know what it was!
And, yet, turmoil swelled inside me for not
having told her about this secret.
I didn't know how to explain it and thought
she might not love me anymore if I tried.

Drugs only brought me temporary relief.
And since I'd been with Janie, I curtailed
my drug use but increased my drinking.
Even though I worked with several guys,
I still felt forsaken and lost in the shop.
And since I seemed to be using my hearing
more and more to aid my failing eyesight,
my *blindness* seemed to worsen whenever
the noise level from machinery increased.
And because I dated the boss' daughter,
I wanted to work hard for Mr. Graber,
but believed my efforts went largely unnoticed,
which only added to my frustration.

Even while my driving skills declined,
I still spent much of my free time with Janie.
Since I drank most days, Janie agreed to drive,
even though she didn't have a license yet.
She loved driving my car, and I loved drinking.
So I kept drinking, and Janie kept driving,
which unriddled my driving dilemma.

A page soon turned in our relationship, however,
when, after dinner one night, the phone rang.
"Hello," I answered. It was Janie.
"What's up?" I asked.
"And don't tell me heaven like ya always do."
"Will you come over and pick me up?
We need to talk," she said grimly.
Uh-oh, I thought, as I said, "I'll be right over."

She met me in her driveway as I pulled in.
"What's the matter?" I asked.
"Just drive," she ordered,
while getting into the passenger's-side seat.

Tears can never be a good sign, I thought,
as she cried while I drove to Fort Smallwood Park,
where we could talk uninterrupted.

"I'm pregnant, Matt. Two months."
She told me as soon as I turned off the engine.
A frightful chill wrapped its arms around me,
like it was December rather than June.
I hugged her and felt warmth, but still wished
I had stopped at the liquor store, before
ever even having picked Janie up.

"I wanted to become Honored Queen
at Job's Daughters. I was next in line," she cried.
"But Honored Queens are supposed to be virgins.
Since pregnancy opposes their moral code,
if I keep this baby, I'm disqualified."
"*If* ya keep the baby? What do ya mean, *if?*
A life is more important than some club!
Please, Janie, tell me ya believe that, too.
All I know is that I love ya and want this baby.
We can get married. And I can start workin'
my way up in your dad's company."

I won't let my blindness mess that up,
I promised myself, as Janie said,

"You're right, Matt. But my parents think otherwise.
You know how involved my father is with the masons
and how important the status of Honored Queen is to him."
"But it's hypocritical, Janie! Can't ya see that?
Even if ya weren't pregnant, you're still not a virgin.
And *that* fact alone disqualifies ya anyway."
"Yeah, but what they don't know won't hurt 'em.
And besides, my parents think I'm too young,

so they want me to get an abortion.
I'm so scared and confused and never told you
that I had an abortion last year,
right after I broke up with Chucky.
And I'm afraid if I have another one,
I won't be able to conceive again."

That *chill* just wrapped its arms around me tighter
than a *Michelin* hugging an auto's rim,
as I sat quietly for a moment,
while soaking up this new revelation
like kitty litter absorbing cat pee!

Had she aborted her other baby
to maintain her status of "purity"
for this club I now hated: Job's Daughters?
Only if I had a Budweiser right now,
I thought to myself. *Think, before ya speak!*

"Look, sweetheart," I said, "The past is the past.
Let's get married and have this child together.
We've already talked about marriage.
We'll just wed sooner rather than later."
"How 'bout October?" She said, as she kissed me.

And that was the last time we'd ever kiss
because her mind soon turned on the matter,
quicker than a weather change on the Chesapeake Bay,
when she decided to abort our baby,
claiming her parents had insisted on it.
I told her I wanted no part of that,
and the blood of our baby was on *her* hands!

* * *

Part Seventeen, Infanticide

"Ya know what, Jenny? I wish I had the cash
to get this bad boy back on the road again.
Whaddya doin'? Oh, snorin'.
I guess between the hash, the weed, and the booze,
it's no surprise you're takin' a snooze.
That bucket seat's rather comfortable, huh?"

It's bubblin'; it's bubblin'; my bong keeps bubblin'!

As more weed scratches the itch in my lungs,
my memories unleash themselves on me;
these beasts lash out at my mind with thorny claws,
taunting me about my RP, and how
Roe v. Wade aided and abetted
in state sanctioned infanticide of my baby.

I guess to try and cheer my sorry butt up,
some friends told me how lucky I was
not to have had to pay for Janie's abortion
like some of them had to pay for their girlfriends'.
For me, it was never about money.
It was about principle. How could I pay
that *hit man*, with M.D. behind his name,
to suck the life from my own flesh and blood?

* * *

Part Eighteen, Busted Again

Soon after Janie *murdered* our baby,
two abbreviations had taken me captive:
PCP and LSD
enlightened my unlit regions with deeper darkness
than booze or weed could ever offer.

Dang, Danny Dumas, late again!
I complained to myself, my patience evaporating
like smoke emanating from an exhaust pipe,
as I waited at The Park for him
and Auggie Bell to arrive with my hit of acid
they promised to bring to me.
Danny had supposedly scored
some butt kickin' acid called *Red Dragon*.

I'm ready to slay it if he ever gets here.

"You're later than a pregnant girl's period,"
I told Danny, after fifteen more minutes had passed,
as he and Auggie stopped beside me.
"Eat a cat turd and die!" Danny countered.
"If you still want the *Red Dragon*, get in."
"Will ya turn the light on, Danny," I asked,
climbing into the backseat of his Vega.
"I'd like to see what the heck I'm buyin'.
What's up, Auggie?" I said, as he looked at me
stone-faced from the front passenger's seat.
"Here's a beer for ya, Matt," Auggie offered.
"Thanks," I said, as I grabbed the opened can.

Auggie never offers anyone a beer,
so why would he give me one, opened even?
Stop being so paranoid, I told myself.

79

As Danny gave me a hit of *Red Dragon,* he said,
"Keep your money. It's on the house."
What's up with all the kindness? I wondered,
until Auggie hollered above The Rolling Stones,
"Can we turn the dang light off now, girls?"

That's more like it, I thought. *Back to normal!*

Placing the small papered piece of acid on my tongue,
I chased it with the lukewarm beer Auggie had given me,
as Danny sped off to a shopping center where we partied.
Within an hour dozens of people had mustered
to get high in the parking lot.
I had dropped acid dozens of times before,
but this time was different from all the rest.
It booked me on a flight I could not cancel,
as that *Dragon* breathed his demonic flame.
And when, like an arsonist, he ignited
the walls of my sanity with his torch,
I saw sounds while people taunted me and said,

It's time for you to die now, Matt. Kill him!
Kill him! It's time for you to die now, Matt!

I saw a police car pull in and thought,
Great! He won't let them kill me. I'm safe now.
But another teenager stepped out from the cruiser
and joined in with the crowd's mantra and said,

It's time for you to die now, Matt. Kill him!
Kill him! It's time for you to die now, Matt!

More voices I saw said,
Here comes the good part.
As the *Dragon* continued his ascent from his lair,

maniacal laughter pierced through my pores
like hypodermic needles, infusing
fiendish tremors throughout my body.
I wrested myself from the madness,
and, yet,
it trailed behind me like a wagon
hitched to my back filled with delirium.

As I tried to escape up Mountain Road,
I felt like a phantom roller skating,
without skates, dodging cars,
whose headlights seemed so close I could touch them
without any physical consequences.
Finally arriving at the Farm Store,
where I once worked,
I stormed through the doors. Meanwhile,
activity massacred my senses with stimulation:
refrigeration from soda coolers roared
like an eighteen-wheeler inside the store,
while ceiling lighting separated into shreds.
Customers stared at me through strange masks.
I needed a dose of night, so I left
and staggered down Janie's darkened road.

As if a demon directed my footsteps,
I stumbled into parked cars, while lights
beaming from porch lamps and windows escorted me
toward my former girlfriend's house.
A car, in the meantime, stopped
and a man said, "Matt, is that you?
What's wrong?"
It was my father.
"Come on, Matt, get in the car. Hurry up!"
But at first I was not convinced it was him, until
the sound of his Galaxie's engine persuaded me.

A woman who knew me from the Farm Store had called
my dad to warn him I was in trouble.

And, later, as I entered through my front door,
my skin felt as if it was slipping from my bones,
believing in my head I had died.
When a fiend usurped my soul from my body,
he brought me to the gates of Hades,
where I saw myself lying in a casket,
my fingers folded as if in prayer.
At the viewing,
my mother clasped my cold hands.
As she wept,
I hovered above the coffin and hollered:
I'm not dead, mom. I'm right here!
As I touched her shoulder, trying to console her,
she did not acknowledge me at all,
still clutching the silent hands of her *dead* son.

A couple of months after my *death,*
Danny Dumas drove me and Auggie Bell
to Annapolis so Auggie could sell
baggies of flakes manufactured in hell,
as "Renegade," by Styx, branded our ears:

The jig is up, the news is out.
They finally found me. The renegade
who had it made retrieved for a bounty.
Never more to go astray.
This'll be the end today of the wanted man,

When Danny turned the wrong way onto Taylor Avenue,
a guardrail on its shoulder stood in its stance
like Dallas' Doomsday defense positioned
on the line of scrimmage ready to sack

our four-wheeled quarterback.
Horns blew from cars, however, instead of from the band,
while *Firestones* screeched rather than applause from fans.
The back of the front passenger's seat halted
my momentum and like a lineman forced me
to fumble my pipe brimming with PCP.

On the wrong side of Taylor Avenue,
beneath a flickering *Bic* butane,
my *Timex* still ticking read 2:10 a.m.
I was stoned with a brain that crackled
like a fire log swallowed up by wretched flame,
as warnings sounded in my mind like sirens:

Toss the dope. Run, Matt, run!

But toss my dope? Nope! I don't think so!
As I loitered by the wreck, shackled
in the shadows of dependency,
PCP and I had no grounds for divorce,
not even a chance for separation,
such were the bonds of my addiction.
While I huddled with the team, Annapolis
dispatched its team, adorned in badges and blue.
And when the jail door slammed shut that night,
I had no idea how long before it might open again.

* * *

Part Nineteen, Pleading My Case

"Baltimore defeats Oakland 4 to 2,
though they needed 12 innings to do it,"
Chuck Thompson exclaims from the radio.

At least they won, though I missed most of the game.

"Ya finally woke up, I see, sleepy head.
Did ya know ya snore like a chainsaw?"
"Shut up, moron!" Jenny chides.
"Did ya know I've been up for ten minutes already
and *you* didn't even know it? What's up with that?
Not payin' attention again, Matt, huh?"

"Whaddya doin', Jenny?" I ask, puzzled.
"I'm writin' a check for ya. What's today's date?"
"It's August 21, 1981."
"It's for the $25.00 ya loaned me last month
to help me pay for my new tires."
"I don't take checks. Put it away, Jenny.
Besides, it wasn't a loan. It was a gift."
And then changing the subject, I say,
while handing over the unoccupied pipe,
"Here! Fill her up with some more hash, will ya?
I gotta find a tree. I'll be right back.
These *Budweisers* went right through me!"

While I was taking care of my business,
guilt like a strong cup of coffee jolted
my conscience awake,
when I saw the Rhododendron bush by my side.
It was a Mother's Day present I stole one day
from a flower stand in Lakeland.
Wasted on Vodka and Valium, I staggered

over to the potted bush, snatched it up,
then looked right into the eyes of the guy,
who worked at overseeing the stand, and said,
"This belongs to my mom. Catch me if ya can!"
Why I'm not in prison I'll never know.

When I get back, Jenny has the bowl cooking.
"I gotta get some of this hash from Tony," I say.
"Do ya wanna play cards later?" Jenny asks.
"Maybe. But first, I gotta find Tony."
"Ya never miss work anymore.
So why did ya take off today?" Jenny asks
for the second time this afternoon.

Why does she keep asking me this?

"I just needed some rest, I guess. Why?"
"It seems like somethin's botherin' ya, that's all."
"Nothin's botherin' me. Leave it alone!"
No way, I'm tellin' her about my blindness.

"Ya never should have gone back to Graber's, Matt."
"Believe me, darlin', when I tell ya,
I'm not gonna get some gold watch
for havin' worked there for 25 years!
I wanna get out of that asbestos dump,
as soon as I can line somethin' else up.
Look, Jenny, after Janie, and that bad
acid trip, my drug bust, and everything else,
I needed some time to tune out alone,
to get my head screwed on straight again.
So after I got my act together,
if ya even wanna call it that,
I went back to work there because I needed
to redeem myself for messin' things up.

85

I was lucky Graber even took me back,
after all the crap that happened with Janie."
"He probably only took ya back because
he wanted ya to get back with Janie.
He knew ya were a better man than that moron
she finally married. What's his name, Marcel?
And what kinda mother names her kid *Marcel*?
And how long did *they* last? A year, wasn't it?"

For some reason Jenny never liked Janie.
Janie knew it, too. I think it was because
Jenny had lived a rough life, while Janie's life,
at least materially, was lavish,
by Pasadena standards, anyway.

"If mom hadn't told ya about her lawyer,
that judge would have marinaded your butt,
then cooked it with a steep prison sentence."
"*Steep* might be an exaggeration, Jenny,
yet, one night in jail, though, was bad enough.
But if Auggie hadn't ditched those baggies,
bulging with *Satan Dust*,
prison would have been our home for a long, long time.
Of course, since they separated us in the jail that night,
after we were arrested,
I never knew, till they released us the next day,
that he had tossed the baggies,
before the cops came and hauled our butts away.
I assumed we had been busted for those, too.
I was so wasted then, Jenny, that nothing made sense.
As I sobered that night,
fear snagged me like sharp fish hooks, biting
through my skin from the inside,
that I'd be the county's houseguest for a while.
I'll never forget that night two years ago in 1979."

"An angel must have been lookin' out for ya,
or some other higher power," Jenny says.
"I do believe God delivered me, somehow.
But for what reason? I have no clue."
"Here, Matt, take the bowl. I'm handin' it to ya."
"I think I've had enough for today, Jenny.
It makes me wanna quit usin' drugs
when I think of the legal mess
I got myself into for chasin' after them.
I had never been more scared than on that day
when I stood before that judge, who could have snatched
my freedom away from me for two years
for possessin' that PCP I refused to toss,
even though I had plenty of chances to have hurled it
as I sat on that guardrail embedded in Danny's car.
And at the trial, knowing full well I was guilty,
I was stunned after the judge dismissed my charges
on a technicality, thanks to your mom's lawyer.
But in hindsight, Jenny, it's clear to me now
that PCP possessed me more than I possessed it."

"I should've kicked Janie's butt for ya, Matt.
That would have been one bruised up Honored Queen,"
Jenny slurs while shadowboxing my windshield.
"Don't be bustin' out my window, Sugar Ray.
That's the *Budweiser* talkin', girl," I say.
"I got your *Budweiser* right here," Jenny quips,
while smacking me in the side of the head.
"I'm so fast ya didn't even see it comin'.
Did ya, mister?" Jenny taunts.

If only ya knew, girl.

* * *

Part Twenty, Saved by Grace

After I slammed the door to my Mustang shut
on that humid night of August 21, 1981,
having mourned enough that day for my RP,
raindrops slid down my windshield like tears.
And over a year later,
tears slid down my face like raindrops
when I learned how spiritual blindness plagued me, too:

A darkness that's painted black with the brush of sin,
darkness denser than the kind RP
could had ever abandoned me in,
a darkness that every human inherited
from the patriarch of our race, Adam, who,
while in the midst of Eden's splendor,
bit freely from fruit God had forbidden,
and, thus, leaving a legacy of death through sin
that kidnapped us from our relationship with our Father,
who loved us so much He sent the second Adam,
Jesus, His Son, to pay our ransom
with the Divine Blood He shed for all
who will repent and call on His name.
After His Father raised Him from the dead,
that Light led multitudes of blind people's feet
onto the path of life everlasting.

I knew the Light was Jesus, who came to save,
yet I still loved darkness rather than the Light—
only because my deeds were evil.
In the eyes of God, whom I had offended,
all have sinned and fallen short of His glory.

O dreaded *Death* where shall we hide from you:
in the philosophies of this world,

or in the promises of politicians,
whether Democratic or Republican,
or in the theories of almighty science,
or in carousing, or in comfort foods,
or in a career, or perhaps in a bank account,
or in a hobby, or in the cares of this life,
or in the arms of a forbidden lover,
or even in the arms of one who's not,
or in watching sports, or in Romance Novels,
or behind a bong or bottle of booze? No!
Only the Blood of Jesus will secure
a place for us in heaven forevermore.

On December 12, 1982,
I began my journey toward my Lord,
but later learned it was His Father, though,
who had been drawing me toward His Son.
On that Sunday morning, six inches of snow
blanketed the earth like a polar bear's hide.
It was the day of my salvation. I knew.
My blind eyes sparkled with sobriety,
and no hangover pounded me either,
which was a bit unusual on a Sunday for me.
I lit up my *Salem.*
Shouldering my way through my front door,
I stepped out onto the ice-packed road,
where flurries gathered swiftly on my hatless hair
that danced a half-foot below my shoulders.
As I lumbered onward to Lake Shore Baptist Church,
I knew full well I needed Jesus.
While peacefulness insulated my soul,
the snow muffled the voices of children
and the rudders of the sleds they steered
deftly between the trees aligning their course
that sloped toward a valley in the woods.

As I trudged along on Mountain Road,
the snowstorm began to hinder my swiftness,
and my body became taut with tension.
Since snow burdened the slim shoulders of the road,
I walked partly in the right lane of the street.
Fearing my chance for salvation was doomed,
it felt as if my soul went a bit berserk.
If I didn't get saved now, would I ever?
I knew if I hurried I'd still have time
to walk the remaining quarter mile to church.
Praying that none of these cars that slithered
along the shifty roadway would crush me
before I received Christ as my Savior,
I paid closer attention than usual because
the wind and the ice and the falling snow
distorted the normal sounds of the street—
sounds I usually leaned on like a staff
that helped to compensate for my loss of sight.

Are churches allowed to close?
If they do, I hope it's not today.

As I crossed through the slush-laden street,
frost bit at my body like a frothing dog.
While I skidded across the parking lot,
scraping sounds from a man shoveling snow
bounced from the bricks of the church.
"Good morning," he said,
steam flowing from his mouth like cigarette smoke.
"Hi! Good mornin'. I was wonderin'.
Do they ever close church?" I asked.
"We wanted to close today. But the pastor said
he believed God wanted us opened.
So enjoy the service."
"I will," I said.

As soon as I set foot inside the door,
my eyes retreated into their *timeout* mode,
as they transitioned to the indoor lighting.
Someone greeted me with a *good morning.*
And since I anticipated a handshake,
I extended mine and was surprised
by a church bulletin instead of a hand.
By the time my eyes cooperated,
the service had already begun.
So I sat in the midst of a desolate pew,
as far away from the pulpit as possible.
As battles, meanwhile, bristled in my mind,
doubts seethed over with things God already resolved.
While swords clashed inside me, vying for my soul,
this verse flashed like neon through my mind:
"Therefore whoever confesses Me before men, him
I will also confess before my Father who is in heaven.
But whoever denies Me before men, him
I will also deny before my Father who is in heaven."
Those words of Jesus sealed the deal, piercing through
a stronghold of cowardice that strangled my heart:
Fear that men might mock had muted my mouth
from proclaiming publicly *Jesus is Lord!*
With the last breath of the sermon breathed out,
I sang along with the congregation:

Just as I am, without one plea,
but that thy blood was shed for me,
and that thou bidst me come to thee,
O Lamb of God, I come, I come!

And when the invitation from the pulpit came,
I sprang from my hellish ditch, dashing
down the aisle toward the front of the church.
"I wanna get saved, pastor," I cried out.

A deacon named Wayne Foy walked over,
shook my hand and led me in a prayer,
in which I repented from my sin,
asking the Lord Jesus to come in.
At that moment I was born again,
God giving me His gift of eternal life.
It felt as if my soul had been swept clean
from the soot that collected there from my sin.

As I headed for home,
relief diffused itself throughout my being,
like after having had an aching tooth pulled.
With the steady crunch of snow beneath my feet,
I neared my house when a soft voice whispered
from somewhere in the depths of my soul, saying:
"I want you to declare My Name in the darkness."
And I responded to Him by saying,
"But *how* do I declare Your Name in darkness, Lord?"

Three decades like a vapor now have passed,
since God gave this blind man's heart some sight.
And even though I'm 99% blind today,
with a 60% hearing loss as well,
God's grace is still sufficient for me,
and His strength is made perfect in my weakness.
And through that grace He cleaned me up
and cured me from my drug-induced disease,
then gave me a pen for a tool to declare
in darkness the name of His Son, Jesus.

"Therefore, if anyone *is* in Christ, *he is* a new creation; old
things have passed away; behold, all things have become
new" (2 Corinthians 5:17).

***

A Gift from God for You

Over thirty years ago I began seeing through blindness once I saw I needed God's Son for the same reason we all do. "For the wages of sin is death; but the gift of God is eternal life through Jesus Christ our Lord" (Romans 6:35). We die because of sin. And what death ultimately means is to be separated from God forever in hell. But because Jesus was fully God and fully Man, and because He loves us, He destroyed death by His resurrection from the dead—after He died on the cross to save us from our sins. This is the gospel. And if we repent from our sins, and believe the gospel, God promises to give us eternal life. And to repent simply means to be sorry to God for our sins, and then turn away from them, and ask His Son, Jesus, to come into our life and forgive us. If you would like to receive God's free gift of eternal life, then pray the prayer below by faith and mean it in your heart.

"Dear Jesus, I know I'm a sinner and would be lost in hell without You. Please forgive me for my sins and come into my life. I believe that You died on the cross for my sins and that God, Your Father, raised You from the dead. Thank You, Jesus, for giving me Your free gift of eternal life. Amen!"

***

Humbling Mistakes Shedding Light on Blindness

During my teenage years and young adult life, the future looked bleak for me after dropping out of high school and delving into drugs. For those reasons if someone back then would have looked into their crystal ball and told me that in the future a college student would write a research paper on a book that I had written, I would have laughed and told them "I hope your warranty hasn't expired because your crystal ball is cracked." But such is the case.

Joseph Andrew Townsend, a film major at Stevenson University in Owings Mills, MD, wrote a research paper last year on *Seeing Through Blindness.* Mr. Townsend said, "I have never seen nor heard of a writer with a degenerative eye disease." In his keen analysis, he unearthed meanings from my book that I did not even know were buried beneath its pages. Mr. Townsend also said that the imagery frequently made him feel like he was in my shoes, adding: "I believe that a book like *Seeing Through Blindness* shows people that they can overcome even the most extreme obstacles." Here is Mr. Townsend's research paper, titled "Humbling Mistakes Shedding Light on Blindness." And, by the way, Mr. Townsend earned an "A" for his work.

Matt Harris's *Seeing Through Blindness* is a captivating autobiography that not only illustrates his struggles with vision loss but also with himself. Written as a narrative poem, Matt refrains from holding back even the most shocking characteristics of his past. The honesty he conveys by presenting his experiences in detail catches interest and appreciation from his audience. Some of the chilling obstacles he is faced with end up shaping the final resolution and his conclusive epiphany. On pages 9-10 [first edition] and again on 85-86 [first edition] the reader

94

is presented with two of Matt's humbling mistakes. Both are from completely different time periods but share common attributes. Despite Matt's lack of sight, he offers a strong visualization of both situations helping the reader conceptualize his surroundings.

In 1971 Matt's vision abnormality was publicly revealed for the first time. It was opening day of his little league baseball season and the stands were packed with spectators. He was playing in right field when, "Lou, batting cleanup, lumbered to the plate" (Harris 9 [first edition]). Knowing he had trouble seeing, Matt prayed that the ball wouldn't end up in his general direction, considering that the bases were loaded. Unfortunately, "God said No to [Matt's] prayer and Yes to Lou Paul's instead." After the pitcher lobbed the ball to the plate, Lou Paul connected with the pitch and it was sent straight towards Matt. As Lou headed for first base, "[Matt] never saw it—not even a glimpse" (Harris 9 [first edition]). Even though he heard the ball hit the fence he couldn't find it, no matter how hard he searched the "grassy bottom" (Harris 9 [first edition]). Nicholas, the first baseman, ran past Matt expressing his frustration by shouting "You moron!" (Harris 9 [first edition]). Due to Matt's humbling mistake, the opposing team scored four runs. Embarrassed, Matt was left standing alone in the outfield "like a blade of grass about to be mown" (Harris 9 [first edition]).

In this passage we are presented with a loss of innocence. Even though Matt is young and participating in a harmless activity nothing can protect him from the harshness of ignorance. His use of imagery is so outstanding that he convinces his audience that they are experiencing this embarrassing situation first hand. Not only does this generate an emotional connection but also a relationship with his readers. To most, Matt's lack of sight would be a disadvantage, but in his case it only strengthens his writing. For example, Matt heavily relies on sound to describe a specific scene, which is displayed when he says, "I heard it, though, rattle the rusty fence" (Harris 9 [first edition]). It is interesting that this description of sound paints a perfect visual illustration for readers, considering it was in no way a visual experience for Matt. In a way his impairment is perfect for writing poetry. He exposes even the simplest of details and turns five-minute altercations into multiple pages of thorough writing. In this particular scenario Matt chooses to reveal his emotions with the use of simile. On lines twenty-nine and thirty of page nine he says, "I swallowed my gum, my pride, and stood alone like a blade of grass about to be mown" (Harris 9 [first edition]). At this point Matt feels separated and perhaps lower than everyone who witnessed his mishap even though there isn't a clinical answer to his problem. This makes the reader realize that the use of the word "mown" is foreshadowing for an unfortunate chain of events.

One of Matt's many unfortunate events is reproduced on page eighty-five [first edition]. He describes driving to Annapolis with his friends Danny Dumas and Auggie Bell to sell "baggies of flakes" (Harris 85 [first edition]). Danny, the driver, ends up going the wrong way down a one-way street and crashes into a guardrail on the side of the road. Matt is impaired from drug abuse and unable to comprehend the significance of the situation. Even though fleeing the scene was a feasible way of avoiding trouble, Matt is "shackled in the shadows of dependency" and chooses to wait by the wreckage (Harris 86 [first edition]). His addiction overcame his reasoning and he ended up getting arrested on controlled substance charges. The passage ends with the cell door "slamming shut" and Matt worried that he won't be released (Harris 86 [first edition]).

Even though Matt's altercation probably took place in a matter of minutes his use of imagery lengthens the duration of the situation. In the first line he describes how, when on a bad LSD trip, he had "died" a few months earlier, signifying the beginning of his substance abuse setbacks. He adds lyrics from the song "Renegade," which foreshadow the wreck that was about to take place. When the guardrail comes into sight Matt seems to bring the scene to a standstill. Using simile he makes the rail seem menacing, "like Dallas's Doomsday defense" (Harris 86 [first edition]). Matt views the situation like it's a football game showing that the drugs are taking a toll on his reasoning. He compares car horns to a marching band, and the screech of tires to applause, perhaps showing that this is more of a game to him than reality. Once again he uses simile to describe the effect the collision had on his body when he says, "[the] seat halted my momentum, and, like a lineman, forced me to fumble my pipe" (Harris 86 [first edition]). The wreck seems to have less of an effect on Matt than the PCP does. Now on the side of the road, Matt describes being "beneath a flickering Bic butane," which shows that despite his predicament he continues to inhale drugs. He is trying to convey his dependency and uses simile again to portray his brain's current state. At this point he is having a mental conversation with himself and is attempting to fight his high. "Toss the dope," he says. "Run, Matt, run!" But invisible chains tie him to the pipe (Harris 86 [first edition]). Unable to leave, Matt unwillingly accepts defeat to not only the authorities but also to the PCP. Once again he's hit rock bottom and uses an image of the cell door closing to show his hopelessness.

The hopelessness Matt experiences in the jail cell is much like that of the baseball field. Even though they are from two completely different time periods, they share very similar attributes. In both passages, Matt can't come up with a solution to his problems and finds himself trapped on both the baseball field as well as behind iron bars. Interestingly enough, both of these humbling mistakes mark the beginning and end of his problems. By uncovering each of these difficult stories Matt has not only provided a lesson for his audience but also admitted to his sins. His poetic approach connects these two scenarios and provides a raw, unedited re-creation of what happened. The honesty and bravery he displays is not only commendable but also inspiring.

Matt Harris is a man who lives by example. Instead of concealing his humbling mistakes he has chosen to capitalize on them, while using faith as a backbone. Despite having a lack of sight Matt said, "I am still seeing through blindness by the light of Jesus." These two passages are edgy and honest. And both of them have the ability not only to help someone with the eye disease Matt was finally diagnosed with, Retinitis Pigmentosa, but also to help anyone struggling with addiction. After reading these two passages you not only have a better understanding of Matt Harris but also of yourself. *Seeing Through Blindness* is like a guide that helps us steer through life's potential obstacles. Even though Matt Harris is a stranger to most of his audience, after reading about his humbling mistakes, he leaves us with a friendship.

36096435R00060

Made in the USA
Middletown, DE
15 February 2019